The 50 Commandments of Commercial Real Estate Investment

THE 50 COMMANDMENTS OF COMMERCIAL REAL ESTATE INVESTMENT

The Vest-Pocket Handbook to Increase Your Intellectual Capital in the Commercial Real Estate Industry

JOSEPH J. ORI

Foreword by Mike Nardini, First Vice President, CBRE Group Inc.

ISBN: 1508859175
ISBN 13: 9781508859178
Library of Congress Control Number: 2015904194
Createspace Independent Publishing Platform
North Charleston, South Carolina

- "Joe has reduced to writing the clear thinking required of today's, and all future, commercial real estate professionals. I hope this becomes required reading for anyone considering our profession or investing in commercial real estate."—Joel Gruber, Vice President, Pacific Southwest Realty Services

- "An excellent book that consistently emphasizes the fact that to be a successful real estate investor, an intimate knowledge of real estate is far more important than the ability to run the numbers."—Peter Susko, Head of Portfolio Management, Swift Real Estate Partners

- "I have handled billions of dollars of real estate transactions for institutional investors and found Joe's book to be knowledgeable and trustworthy and provides an extensive background in commercial real estate."—Frank Jansen, Senior Vice President, Chicago Title and Trust Company

- "Whether you are a new investor in commercial real estate or a seasoned veteran, you will find Joseph Ori's new book, *The Fifty Commandments of Commercial Real Estate Investment*, to be both informative and insightful. I consider his book to be a must-have reference guide for successful investment in the commercial real estate sector. Not only knowing but also thoroughly understanding his fifty commandments will make anyone a much wiser investor in commercial property."—Joel W. Hiser, Chief Executive Office, HTL Hospitality Advisors

ACKNOWLEDGMENTS

I WOULD LIKE TO acknowledge these individuals for their assistance in writing this book. First is my childhood friend and commercial real estate colleague, Mike Nardini, first vice president of CBRE Group Inc., Urban Land Advisory, Chicago, for his diligence and thoughtful words in preparing the Foreword to this book. Second is my good friend and one of the best commercial real estate developers I know, Russ Posey, principal, Real Estate Advisory Services, Legacy Consulting Group, Atlanta, for editing the manuscript for this book. Their thoughts, comments, and suggestions were invaluable.

FOREWORD

I HAVE KNOWN JOE Ori since elementary school in a suburb of Chicago. We have tested each other all the way from the day we met through graduate school and continually throughout our business careers. Joe and I have always shared a keen interest in micro- and macroeconomic factors related to real estate and the economy. We have enjoyed what we have both learned from our different vantage points—architecture, investment banking, real estate development, construction, finance, marketing, and brokerage—and have tried to apply the lessons in our real estate practices.

I have been anxiously waiting for Joe to complete this book. I think he hit home on many of these commandments. Joe has a unique qualification to pen this treatise. He has worked inside the financial infrastructure of the commercial real estate industry and watched from the inside through two major economic meltdowns, twenty years apart.

The first meltdown began in Texas in the mid-1980s when the oil and real estate industries collapsed, and the second meltdown happened twenty years later when the entire economy collapsed in the Great Recession of 2007. I wish I would have listened more closely to Joe in 2006 when he was screaming about the inverted yield curve and the impending market bust. He would have saved me millions. I love the fact that this new book is a "vest-pocket" book, and I will carry it with me. As a matter of fact, I work for the largest real estate organization on earth, and I think many in the organization would benefit from reading this. A concept such as the capitalization rate is often misunderstood in our business, but Joe's explanation of it is insightful and easy to understand, and it deserves to be memorized. His doses of sarcasm add a lighter side to some very serious issues and make the book both fun to read and easy to remember.

I love his commandment fourteen, where he warns of buying below replacement cost only if the income approach is higher. I hope to carry that one with me.

Two of my favorite sections in the book are his four different NOIs and his comparisons of actual performance versus acquisition pro formas. Great stuff.

I am also an avid reader of Joe's monthly commercial real estate newsletter, *View of the Market*, and a faithful student of anything he writes about yield curves.

I recommend this book with high regard if you invest in real estate assets or are in the commercial real estate industry, and I hope you carry this in your vest pocket.

Mike Nardini
First Vice President
Urban Land Advisory
CBRE Group Inc.
Chicago

PREFACE

*T*HE FIFTY COMMANDMENTS *of Commercial Real Estate Investment* is a book I have wanted to write for a number of years. It is a concise compendium of important and somewhat comical directives and commandments learned during my thirty-five years of experience in the industry. The commandments are serious, satirical, critical, and funny. They hold a wealth of information in the form of dos and don'ts, tips, mistakes, successes, and strategies for becoming a better and more successful real estate professional.

These commandments should be learned by every commercial real estate practitioner from the young, new real estate broker to the cagey industry veteran. This easy-to-read book should be on the desk of every experienced real estate professional as well as the college graduate seeking his or her first job with a commercial real estate firm.

The areas that are covered include commercial real estate investment, finance, development, capital markets, management, strategies, institutional investment, leasing, financial analysis, and all property types, including apartments, office buildings, shopping centers, industrial warehouses, lodging properties, and senior-housing properties.

Joseph J. Ori
Walnut Creek, California
Spring 2015

INTRODUCTION

I N WRITING THIS vest-pocket book, I have tried to distill, in an understand-able way fifty commandments of commercial real estate investment. Each commandment is listed along with explanations, analysis, and examples, where warranted, to provide a thorough and easy-to-read presentation.

I began my career in commercial real estate in 1981 in Chicago as con-troller at a start-up real estate syndicator by the name of VMS Realty, Inc. I was about the fifteenth person hired at the firm, primarily to create an ac-counting system for the multitude of commercial real estate deals the firm was acquiring. This was great experience and cemented the beginning of my thirty-five-year journey in and love of the commercial real estate business. After VMS, I had various senior-level positions in commercial real estate fi-nance, investments, investment banking, advisory services, and management. I currently own a commercial real estate advisory firm, Paramount Capital Corporation, located in Walnut Creek, California. I am a certified public accountant (nonactive), chartered financial analyst, and adjunct professor of finance at Santa Clara University. I also hold an MBA in finance and publish a commercial real estate newsletter, *View of the Market*. My website is www. paramountcapitalcorp.com.

During my career, I have been involved in over $3.2 billion in transactions, including acquisitions, financings, joint ventures, advisory assignments, lever-age buyouts, development transactions, and property management. Along the way, I have had the ups and downs of a roller coaster, but the experience and learning have been invaluable. My journey in the industry is still ongoing, and

I am still learning new and clever strategies and tricks. Hopefully, I will be able to share these new opportunities in a second book down the road.

Joseph J. Ori
Walnut Creek, California
Spring 2015

COMMANDMENT 1

Acquiring commercial real estate at low capitalization rates significantly increases the odds that the equity investors will eventually lose their capital.

O NE OF THE most important investment metrics of commercial real estate (CRE) is the capitalization rate, or the net operating income from a property divided by the property's value or purchase price. The net operating income is a property's gross potential rent less vacancy plus other income less operating expenses, excluding depreciation and interest expense. The net operating income is a cash-basis number. The higher the capitalization rate, the lower the property value, and the lower the capitalization rate, the higher the property value. The capitalization rate may also be determined by the following formula:

Risk-free rate of return (Rrf) plus a CRE risk premium (Rp) less the rental-growth rate (G), or the following:

$$Rrf + Rp - G$$

The risk-free rate of return is based on US Treasury securities, typically the ten-year T-Note, which today is about 2 percent. US Treasury securities are used as the risk-free rate because the risk of default is almost zero. The United States is the largest economy and has the most liquid capital markets in the world. The CRE risk premium is harder to determine, as there is very little research or empirical evidence on the risk premium. Commandment forty-four, page 88 discusses fifteen CRE risks, and these would be the foundation for the projected risk premium. In my experience in the CRE industry, the risk premium has been between 3 percent and 10 percent; for this analysis, we will use 8 percent. The growth rate is the projected growth in rent or income for the property; for this analysis, we will use 2.5 percent. Therefore, the general capitalization rate today would be 2 percent plus 8 percent minus 2.5 percent, or 7.5 percent. This capitalization rate needs to be adjusted up or down by increasing or decreasing the risk premium and the growth rate depending on the type of property, location, tenancy, and quality of the property.

A property with a net operating income of $1.2 million and a capitalization rate of 7.5 percent would yield a value of $16 million ($1.2 million/7.5 percent). With a lower capitalization rate of 5 percent, the value is $24 million ($1.2 million/5 percent). Therefore, the higher the capitalization rate, the lower the value, and the lower the capitalization rate, the higher the value. During the boom and easy-credit period from about 2004 through 2007 (before the Great Recession) and beginning again in 2014 through today, capitalization rates have compressed to dangerously low and uneconomical levels. Most of this has been the result of the Federal Reserve's zero-interest-rate policy, which reduced short-term interest rates. This program has compressed capitalization rates, reduced the cost of capital, and raised real estate asset prices. This policy has also created distortions in the capital markets by mispricing debt and equity capital. Many class-A apartment properties are trading at ridiculously low capitalization rates of between 3.5 percent and 4.5 percent. Class-A leased office buildings in twenty-four-hour cities such as New York, San Francisco, Miami, and Boston are also trading at nosebleed capitalization rates of 4 percent to 5 percent.

Acquiring CRE at low capitalization rates is one of the main reasons CRE deals underperform and investors earn low returns or lose their equity capital. This is especially the case in the current zero-interest-rate environment, wherein rates can't go any lower and will most likely rise in the next few years. A CRE property bought at a low 4 percent capitalization rate and sold years later at a higher capitalization rate will result in the investors earning a single-digit return or losing some of their equity in the property. For example, suppose a $10 million property is acquired with $7 million interest-only debt at 4.25 percent and $3 million in investor equity. The property is held for five years, and the net operating income increases by 5 percent per year. The property is sold at the end of year five by applying a 6 percent capitalization rate (higher than the purchase capitalization rate due to a higher-interest-rate environment) to the year-six net operating income. Under this financial scenario, the internal rate of return to the equity investor is only 4.1 percent, and if the income growth is less than 5 percent and the capitalization rate is higher than 6 percent, the investor would have lost a portion of his or her equity investment.

There's an old saying in CRE: you make money when a property is bought, not when it is sold. This means that properties must be bought at appropriate risk-adjusted capitalization rates. Failure to do so will most likely result in losses.

COMMANDMENT 2

Sometimes, a higher and better use is to sell it to someone else.

THIS COMMANDMENT IS a sarcastic statement on the higher-and-better-use concept. The higher and better use is a CRE-appraisal term that refers to the most valuable use of a specific piece of land or property. The highest and best use of a property has four basic criteria:

1. Physically achievable. Any potential use must be physically possible given the size, shape, topography, and other characteristics of the site.
2. Legally allowable. The use of the property must conform to local zoning laws and any deed restrictions and covenants.
3. Highest productivity. The property must generate the highest return to the owner or developer.
4. Financially feasible. The property must generate an adequate return on the financial investment to justify the costs of acquiring or constructing the physical asset plus a profit for the developer or owner.

The highest and best use of most existing properties meets all of the criteria above. However, the highest and best use of a property may change over time. These changes are usually due to economic changes in the local market; demographic changes in incomes, race, employment, and so on; outmigration of the population for an area; or changes in zoning laws by the local municipality. Also, the current financial feasibility may become uneconomical due to the net operating income from the property not providing a suitable economic return on the property investment to the owner. For example, an area that has been the site of high-rise low-income housing may be gentrified into low-rise apartments and townhomes; a former location of an office building may get a zoning change to allow for development of an apartment complex; or a gas-station site may be developed into an office building.

Changes in the highest and best use of CRE occur frequently. Many times, the property owner has no control over the change. If a property owner does foresee a negative change in the highest and best use, then it may be time to sell it to someone else.

COMMANDMENT 3

**You suffer from knowing the numbers. The more
you know about capitalization rates, cash flow, value,
returns, and so on, the fewer properties you will buy.**

THIS CYNICAL COMMANDMENT refers to the situation when experienced
CRE investors have a difficult time buying properties because they know
so much about the real estate business that they have difficulty agreeing to the
sellers' high prices. This knowledge base comes with many years of experience
in buying, selling, financing, and developing properties. The more savvy a
real estate professional becomes over time about property values, costs, capitalization rates, internal rates of return, financing, operations, capital markets,
boom and bust markets, and so on, the harder it is to complete transactions.

Acquiring CRE is a difficult business and requires persistence, patience,
and a lot of time chasing potential deals. In boom periods, most properties
placed on the market for sale are overpriced by 20 percent or more, and it's
difficult to agree to a sales transaction with the seller. This is why you suffer
from knowing the numbers. The more a real estate executive knows about the
CRE business, the fewer deals he or she will complete.

COMMANDMENT 4

**Diversification by property, location, and industry
is a commercial real estate owner's best friend.**

THIS COMMANDMENT REFERS to lowering the risk of owning CRE investment by diversifying a portfolio by the four main property types—office buildings, multifamily apartments, industrial warehouses, and shopping centers—as well as by location and industry concentration. The universe of the different types of CRE investments is shown in the four-quadrant chart below. The chart is divided based on whether the investments are public or private and equity or debt. Most institutional investors or large real estate funds use this four-quadrant analysis to develop their CRE-investment strategy. Once the investment strategy is developed, the portfolio should be further diversified by property type, location, and industry.

	Public	Private
Equity	REITs REOCs (real estate operating companies)	Direct acquisitions Joint ventures Commingled/special-account funds Private-equity real estate funds Nontraded REITs Closed-end funds
Debt	CMBS (commercial mortgage-backed securities)	First mortgages Mezzanine loans Subordinate loans Bridge loans Participating loans

In the investment world, there are two types of risk: systematic risk and nonsystematic risk. Systematic risk refers to risk that affects everyone, such as higher-interest rates, high inflation, loose credit, and a national recession. Nonsystematic risk is company- or property-specific risk, such as bankruptcy of a major tenant, negative demographic changes in the local market, and loss of a major institutional investor. See commandment forty-four on page 88 for my list of the fifteen CRE risks.

Because systematic risk affects the entire economy, it cannot be eliminated and must be absorbed by CRE investors. Nonsystematic risk, however, can be eliminated by diversification of a portfolio by property type, location, and industry. Public real estate investment trusts (REITs) are primarily one-property-type companies and do not diversify by property type. This has been the case since the early 1990s and stems from the Wall Street analyst community that is reluctant to analyze multiple property types under one entity. Investors who buy individual REIT stocks can easily diversify by buying multiple REITs with different property types or invest in a multi-REIT mutual fund or exchange-traded fund (ETF).

This commandment primarily applies to institutional property owners, sponsors, and investors who own or invest in large funds or portfolios of CRE throughout the country. The best way to reduce the nonsystematic risk of a portfolio is to diversify the portfolio by property type and location. The final diversification strategy that is often overlooked by CRE investors is diversification by industry or having a low industry concentration as tenants. Many CRE investors do not review and analyze what industries account for a high percentage of tenants or employment for their properties. For example, the majority of tenants in office and industrial buildings in San Jose and Silicon Valley are in the technology industry, and if that industry goes into a downturn, it could increase vacancies dramatically for these properties. Apartments in the same technology-infused area may rent to tenants, the majority of whom also work in the technology industry, which, again, increases this concentration risk. Therefore, it is critical to diversify a large CRE portfolio by property, location, and industry concentration to increase returns and lower risk.

COMMANDMENT 5

I would rather own a class-B property in an A location than a class-A property in a B location.

ONE OF THE longtime axioms of real estate is location, location, location. A great location is a key attribute of a good and valuable CRE property. As discussed in commandment two on page 4, the highest and best use of a property is the one that provides the highest value. In many cases, it is the location and land value that allow the property on the site to generate premium rents, resulting in a higher valuation. Most CRE properties are informally rated as being class A (the premium property in the market), class B (an average property in the market), or class C (the worst or least desirable property in the market).

If the location and land value is instrumental in the property earning high rents, then owning a class-B property in an A location will almost always be a better CRE investment than a class-A property in a B location. If a parcel of real estate is in a mediocre or poor location, then it won't matter if the property on the site is new or has great amenities, as it will not be able to realize high rents and hence high value.

There are two ways to determine the intrinsic value of a CRE property. The first method, as discussed in commandment one, is to apply the capitalization rate to the net operating income to derive a value. The other method is to calculate a discounted cash flow to the equity investors using a weighted-average cost of capital for the property. A class-B property in an A location will, as stated above, provide for higher rents and therefore a higher value as compared with a class-A property in a B location.

A class-B property in an A location has a competitive advantage that provides a buffer or "moat" around the property. This advantage means that it will be very difficult for competitors to enter the market with a similar type of property and location to extract some of the premium rents from the class-B property. The owner of the class-B property on the A site may, if financially feasible, demolish and rebuild or renovate the property to bring the physical building up to class-A standards. In any case, it is always more profitable to own a class-B property in an A location than a class-A property in a B location.

COMMANDMENT 6

It's better to buy good real estate at a great value than to buy great real estate at a good value.

ONE OF THE key objectives of a successful CRE investment is buying property at a great value. Many real estate investors do just the opposite. They buy a good or great property but at a high price and low capitalization rate that is a poor value. The value of the real estate is more important than the quality of the asset. To earn the greatest return from a piece of real estate, it must be purchased at a great value, which means at a price and risk-adjusted capitalization rate that are attractive and profitable.

A 95 percent leased, one-million-square-foot, class-A office building located on Fifth Avenue in New York purchased for $2,000 per square foot and a 4 percent capitalization rate by an institutional investor will be heralded as a great deal. Although this may be a great property to show your investors and include on the cover of your company brochure, it is not a good value. The price is too high, and the capitalization rate is too low, and although the property may be resold in a few years at an even higher price, it will eventually be repriced down, based on a normal capitalization rate and return. Alternatively, a two-hundred-thousand-square-foot, class-A office building purchased in Tucson, Arizona, at an 8 percent capitalization rate and $300 per square foot is good real estate at a great value.

Most institutional investors, such as pension funds, insurance companies, and sovereign-wealth funds, follow the herd in CRE investing just as they do when buying public equities. They are very risk averse and will bid with twenty other institutional investors to buy the New York building at an overpriced 4 percent capitalization rate. However, they will not buy the Tucson building that is available at the significantly higher 8 percent risk-adjusted return because it's in a smaller market and doesn't have the pizzazz of a major New York City office building. The CRE executives who manage these institutional investment firms also won't get fired or reprimanded if they buy the New York building and lose money. This is because all their competitors are also heavily invested in New York, buying similar buildings. Since they will also suffer property losses, everyone is in the same boat, and no one will be terminated. If the same institutions bought the Tucson building, and the property falters and they lose money, their jobs will be at risk for investing in a second-tier property market.

COMMANDMENT 7

All the bad news (bankruptcies, fraud, foreclosure, lawsuits, and so on) in commercial real estate comes out when the economy tanks.

WHEN THE ECONOMY and CRE industry are booming, everyone in the industry is making money, and there is very little bad news emanating from disagreements, lawsuits, bad deals, foreclosures, fraud, and so on. The bad news that plagues the CRE industry usually comes out when the economy tanks, typically from a bad recession or tight credit conditions. The CRE industry, which is cyclical by nature through its dependence on economic growth and favorable capital markets, is heavily impacted by a recessionary environment.

The five-year period from 2002 to 2006 and before the Great Recession, which was from 2007 through 2012, was a boom time for the CRE and housing industries. In 2002, the Federal Reserve had just reduced short-term interest rates to 1 percent, coming off the dot-com recession, and the real estate business took off. There were dramatic increases in CRE transactions, including sales, financings, and leases, and the production of single-family homes, to the tune of more than one million units per year. There was also a booming business of securitizing subprime home loans. Beginning in 2007, the overheated housing market began to contract, and a number of residential mortgage banking and subprime lending firms, such as New Century

Financial, Ownit Mortgage Solutions, and Mortgage Lenders Network, defaulted on their obligations and went bankrupt. This led to a domino effect and the collapse of the housing, banking, CRE, investment banking, and financial industries.

As the CRE industry continued to deteriorate in 2007 and beyond, all the bad news of the industry became public. This included numerous bankruptcies, frauds in real estate lending, foreclosures of real estate projects by banks, defaults of commercial mortgage-backed security loans, disagreements among joint-venture partners, and thousands of lawsuits. The plethora of lawsuits included investors suing sponsors for lost equity funds, joint-venture partners suing each other over failed investments, banks suing borrowers for defaulted loans, subordinate lenders suing property owners for payment, and brokers suing principals for unpaid fees and commissions.

To quote Warren Buffett, "Only when the tide goes out do you discover who's been swimming naked." It is the same in the CRE industry. In boom times, industry participants are happy making money and doing multiple transactions, but when the economy turns down, all the bad news comes out, and the industry continues to deteriorate.

COMMANDMENT 8

**It takes twenty years to build a great reputation
in the commercial real estate industry but
only one bad deal to tarnish it.**

A GOOD REPUTATION IS key to being a successful real estate participant.
A good reputation can open doors for good properties to sell, lease, or
broker and will make it easier to develop or acquire CRE assets. It is also
much simpler to obtain financing for a firm that has a good reputation in the
marketplace. Investors and lenders will more likely invest with or lend their
funds to a firm that has a good reputation in the industry, and this will be
based on the firm's track record of investment returns, quality of property and
asset management, and treatment of capital providers.

However, it usually takes just one bad deal to tarnish a reputation. One
of the best examples is Blackrock Real Estate, a unit of Blackrock Inc., the
largest investment manager in the world with more than $4 trillion under
investment. Blackrock Real Estate is a unit of Blackrock Inc., which invests in
commercial real estate and REITs through direct investments and various real
estate funds. In 2006, Blackrock partnered with Tishman Speyer Properties, a
New York–based CRE-development firm, to acquire Stuyvesant Town–Peter
Cooper Village apartment complex in New York City.

The apartment complex is an 11,232-unit apartment village in 110 buildings, built on eighty acres, located at First Avenue between Fourteenth through

Twentieth Streets and was built by Metropolitan Life in the 1940s. The partners acquired the complex from Metropolitan Life for a contract price of $5.4 billion and a total cost with fees and improvement costs of approximately $6.3 billion. Each of the partners invested $112.500 million and promoted the project to other equity investors for a 13.5 percent internal rate of return. The capitalization rate on the deal was 2.5 percent due to many of the units being under rent control. The acquisition was structured with a first mortgage of $3 billion, thirteen levels of mezzanine debt totaling $1.4 billion, and fifteen equity investors, including the sponsors investing $1.889 billion. The investment group defaulted on the first mortgage in 2010, a mere four years after purchase, and the complex was taken over by the special servicer of the securitized first mortgage, CW Capital. Upon foreclosure, all the equity and mezzanine investments were wiped out at a total loss of $3.3 billion. Many of the mezzanine lenders and equity investors were brought into the deal by Tishman and Blackrock, and when their funds were lost, the sponsors of the deal were tarred and feathered as sophomoric and unsophisticated in commercial real estate investment. The head of one sponsor's real estate business unit was forced to retire, and the reputation of the firm from a commercial real estate perspective has been stained ever since. The acquisition and financing of the Stuyvesant Town–Peter Cooper Village apartment complex was one of the worst commercial real estate deals ever.

COMMANDMENT 9

The most successful real estate chief executive officers surround themselves with people who are smarter than they are.

MANY CRE EXECUTIVES, whether chief executive officers (CEOs) or managing partners, started out as entrepreneurial businesspeople who built up their companies from scratch or from one-room real estate operations. Some started out as real estate brokers, and others worked for a real estate private-equity firm or developer. When the time was right, they went off on their own, sometimes with a partner or two, and started building an organization. Many of today's most successful real estate firms began this way, including Sam Zell's Equity Group Investments, Donald Trump's Trump Organization, and Steve Schwartzman's Blackstone Group. These investors have great entrepreneurial talent, real estate smarts, drive to create profitable companies, and focus to become successful in the very challenging business of CRE. One other important trait these and other successful CRE executives have is hiring and surrounding themselves with young, bright, and aggressive employees who are smarter than the executives are. Mark Zuckerberg, the billionaire founder and CEO of Facebook, was recently asked what type of people he hires. His answer was, "I only hire people who I would work for."

However, many CRE executives do just the opposite when hiring employees and building an organization. They hire people who are not as smart as they are, who they can dominate, or who are proverbial yes-people. They are insecure about themselves and their business acumen, and they don't want to be challenged on their decisions and modus operandi. During my career, I have worked for both successful and unsuccessful and insecure CEOs, and the ones who were the best to work for surrounded themselves with smart people. The most important assets in any real estate organization, or any company for that matter, are its employees and their intellectual capital. An organization will not grow and prosper without hiring knowledgeable and high-quality personnel with a diverse set of skills that contribute to the growth and prosperity of the company. In the CRE industry, if you don't take care of your people, they will leave, form their own companies, and become your competitors.

COMMANDMENT 10

There is a negative correlation between the fees to the general partner or sponsor of a deal and the internal rate of return to the limited partners.

A LMOST EVERY CRE investment or development requires outside equity capital to complete the capitalization of the property. To obtain this capital, the sponsor or general partner of the deal prepares a private-placement memorandum (PPM) or prospectus to provide prospective equity investors with information on the deal during the capital-raising process. The PPM typically includes information on the real estate investment strategy, property or properties to be acquired, use of investor proceeds, ownership structure, background and biographies on the sponsors, tax information, and other property-related data. Depending on the type of deal, the fees, or load, to the sponsor and firm selling the deal can be 2 percent to 13 percent of the equity capital raised. For example, if the equity raised is $50 million, then the fees may range from $1 million (2 percent) for an institutional deal to $6.5 million (13 percent) for a private real estate investment trust or commingled fund.

The higher the fee structure, the more difficult it will be to deliver an acceptable return to the investors. A deal with a load of 13 percent means that only 87 percent of the capital raised will be invested in the real estate assets. The chart below compares the internal rate of return on two real estate investments with a gross equity raise of $50 million. The capitalization rate of 7 percent is identical, and the only differences are that investment A has an upfront load of 2 percent and can acquire more property with the same leverage, and investment B has a higher upfront load of 13 percent and must acquire less property.

	Investment A: 2 percent Load	Investment B: 13 percent Load
Gross equity raise	$50,000,000	$50,000,000
Less fees and costs	($1,000,000)	($6,500,000)
Net equity investment in the property	$49,000,000	$43,500,000
Purchase price of property	$147,000,000	$130,500,000
First mortgage, interest only, at 5 percent	$98,000,000	$87,000,000
Investor equity investment	$49,000,000	$43,500,000
Property capitalization	$147,000,000	$130,500,000
Net operating income: year one	$10,290,000	$9,135,000
Capitalization rate	7%	7%
Annual net operating-income growth (five-year investment period)	2.5%	2.5%
Terminal capitalization rate	7%	7%
Internal rate of return to the equity investors	16.9%	13.6%

As shown in the table, investment A has a low fee structure of 2 percent and delivers a higher internal rate of return of 16.9 percent, while investment B, with the higher fee structure at 13 percent, earns a lower internal rate of return of 13.6 percent. This simple analysis indicates the negative correlation between the fees to the sponsor or general partner and the investor.

COMMANDMENT 11

There is at least one formula error in every large and complicated Excel underwriting spreadsheet.

To PROPERLY ANALYZE a CRE investment or development, an Excel spreadsheet or Argus-type software program must be used to create the proforma analysis. The pro forma will usually be for five, seven, or ten years and include a detailed financial analysis over the selected period. The analysis will include each tenant and his or her base rent plus other income and expense reimbursements; operating expenses such as real estate taxes, insurance, utilities, repairs and maintenance, advertising, marketing, management fees and salaries, tenant improvements, leasing commissions, capital improvements, principal and interest on the debt; and the cash flow to the equity investors.

Most real estate firms and their senior analysts take great pride in developing these very sophisticated Excel spreadsheets to analyze potential real estate acquisitions and developments. Some of the spreadsheets I've seen have up to ten separate subworksheets. Many of these Excel works of art contain sophisticated formulas, macros, pivot tables, and other complicated computations. As great as these spreadsheets are, there is usually at least one error in one of the numerous formulas, which may make the entire analysis almost worthless and the investor returns erroneous. I've seen spreadsheets that concluded that the return on equity to the investors was 18 percent when it was really less than 10 percent. This was due to an error in the internal rate-of-return formula that did not properly calculate the preferred return and repayment of the investor's equity.

Anyone who prepares one of these complicated Excel spreadsheets should have someone else review the formulas to make sure they are correct and the logic of the analysis makes sense. This will prevent senior management from relying on a spreadsheet with erroneous data and conclusions and making a poor investment decision.

COMMANDMENT 12

Price is what a real estate deal costs; value is what you create.

THIS COMMANDMENT IS somewhat related to commandment six, page 12, "It's better to buy good real estate at a great value than great real estate at a good value." The price paid for a CRE asset is what a property costs. Typically, this price includes the purchase price, closing fees and costs, and required capital expenses and improvements to the property. However, value is what is created during the ownership of the real estate asset. How is this value created? First, by buying the property at a good price; second, by executing a positive strategic plan for the ownership of the property; and third, by being highly disciplined in the management and leasing of the property to increase occupancy, revenue, and net operating income and to lower expenses and reduce debt.

One of the most critical steps in creating value has to do with the property-management and leasing functions. Property management involves the on-site management of the property; dealing with tenants' issues; and paying property-level expenses such as real estate taxes, insurance, repairs and maintenance, utilities, and advertising and management fees. Property management also includes determining market rents, negotiating leases with new and existing tenants, and—maybe the most important aspect—delivering the highest level of customer service.

Apartment properties are usually managed by the owner of the property, although some owners hire third-party management companies to perform the on-site management function. Many commercial properties, such as office buildings, shopping centers, and industrial warehouses, will hire a third-party brokerage firm such as CBRE, Jones Lang Lasalle, or Cushman & Wakefield as the leasing agent for the property, while the owner provides the on-site management.

Creating value in a CRE property is very difficult, and the best way to do so is through high-quality property management and leasing. These two functions are the operational side of CRE ownership and are downplayed or ignored in many real estate firms. However, they must be made a priority as creating value equates to higher returns to investors and owners. The most successful CRE-investment firms and developers excel at property management and leasing that leads to superior value creation.

COMMANDMENT 13

If your real estate deal is underperforming, hold it for another five years until the next commercial real estate bull market, and then sell it.

THIS IS ANOTHER satirical commandment that comments on the cyclicality and volatility of the economy and the CRE industry. Since the 1960s, the CRE industry has gone through eight recessions, including two secular downturns. The first secular downturn occurred from 1987 to 1992 and was the result of the Tax Reform Act of 1986 that lengthened depreciation schedules for CRE and curtailed the practice of all real estate investors being able to deduct 100 percent of real estate losses. The second secular downturn began in 2007 and ended in 2012. This downturn, known as the Great Recession, was caused by the drop in housing prices, frothy increase in all asset prices, oversecuritization of subprime home loans and other assets, and misguided government policy that all Americans should own a home.

The volatility of the CRE industry has gotten much worse over the decades, with the down or recessionary periods lasting longer and being deeper and the up or boom periods becoming shorter. This has created a short-term-hold mentality in the industry. Thirty years ago, it was common for institutional investors to buy and hold a property for seven to ten years or more, with the average holding period being about eight years. CRE was an appreciating asset that provided inflation protection and increasing value. During the last decade or so, the average holding period has been reduced to somewhere around three years. This has been the result of the get-rich-quick mentality, short-term investment horizon of equity investors, volatile capital markets, and zero-interest-rate policy of the Federal Reserve. The Fed's zero-interest-rate policy has been the most important reason for the short-term holding period during the last few years. As interest rates have been driven to zero, capitalization rates have followed to unrealistic and dangerously low levels. Investors are reluctant to buy and hold property at these capitalization rates for long periods because they are afraid of rising interest rates, which in turn increase capitalization rates, with the cascade effect of a dramatic reduction in the terminal sales value of the property.

Properties that are not performing well due to high vacancies, lower rents, and negative changes in the local market in most cases cannot be sold at realistic prices. The sellers must hold on to the properties until at least the next CRE bull market, hoping for a repeat of prior-cycle sins, and then unload the project.

COMMANDMENT 14

**Buying property below replacement cost is great
but only if the value of the property per the
income approach is the same or higher.**

MANY REAL ESTATE investment firms tout that the property they are
buying is a great value because it is being purchased below replacement cost. Replacement cost in CRE refers to the cost to build a building of
the same quality and functional utility as the subject property. Obviously,
acquiring a property below replacement cost is great and has historically in-
dicated that the buyer found a "great deal." Competitors in the market that
own or are building a similar property will not be able to compete with the
below-replacement-cost property because their investment objectives will not
allow for lower rents or other financial concessions needed to capture or retain
tenants. With its lower cost basis, the replacement-cost property will have a
competitive rent advantage that will allow the owner to gain market share,
improve financial performance, and create value in the property.

There is one problem with the buy-below-replacement-cost scenario, and
that is that it only makes sense if the value of the property established pursuant
to the income approach is greater. The income approach refers to the method-
ology of using the direct-capitalization approach or the discounted cash-flow
approach in determining the value of a property. Direct capitalization is an
appraisal method of applying a capitalization rate (see commandment one

on page 1) to the property's net operating income to calculate its value. The discounted cash-flow approach is also an appraisal method that discounts a property's net operating income or cash flow after debt at an acceptable discount rate to calculate its value.

There are cases during distressed periods when a property may be purchased below replacement cost, but this price is higher than the value determined using the income approach as discussed above. Therefore, it would not be a good value. This situation usually happens when there is a secular downturn in the economy and industry as happened in the Great Recession from 2007 to 2012. During this period, the value of many CRE properties fell precipitously due to declining rents and occupancies as well as the lack of debt and equity capital. The value of most properties during this period fell far below replacement cost; however, the income approach produced an even lower value. Therefore, investors must understand that buying a property below replacement cost is great but only if that value is equal to or less than the value determined by the income approach.

COMMANDMENT 15

**In every commercial real estate acquisition, there are
four different net operating incomes: the seller's actual
and pro forma and the buyer's actual and pro forma.**

I N THE CRE-ACQUISITION process, there are four different net operating incomes (NOIs) in the transaction. The NOI is a property's gross potential rent less vacancy plus other income less operating expenses excluding depreciation and interest expense. The seller provides two different NOIs. One is the actual NOI for the prior year or period, and the other is the pro-forma NOI for the next period. The actual NOI is usually redacted to exclude operating expenses that the seller believes are not relevant to owning/managing the property and should be disregarded by the buyer. The seller's pro-forma NOI is typically included in the sales package prepared by the seller and his or her sales broker. The future projected NOI is always substantially greater than the actual NOI for current and prior periods, as it usually includes lower expenses and reduced management fees and anticipates all vacant space leased up to achieve a 95 percent or higher occupancy.

The purchaser in the transaction also has two different NOIs. The first one is the purchaser's modification of the seller's actual NOI with adjustments for expenses such as repairs and maintenance, management fee, and vacancy in accordance with the purchaser's property-management and ownership strategy. The purchaser's second NOI is the pro-forma NOI based on the buyer's objectives and strategy in leasing and managing the property for the next year.

Since there are four difference NOIs, which one is the most important to the potential purchaser? Both of the purchaser's NOIs are important, but the pro-forma NOI is the most important and should be used to determine the offer price and capitalization rate of the property. The modified actual NOI for the current year reveals to the buyer what the real income, operating expenses, and NOI are, as if the property was operated by the purchaser. The pro-forma NOI is used by the purchaser to determine the acquisition price that he or she is comfortable in paying for the property and is based on the modified actual NOI and desired capitalization rate. The purchaser's pro-forma NOI will be significantly less than the seller's pro-forma NOI due to more conservative and realistic underwriting criteria and assumptions. The seller's NOI is almost always based upon an exuberant leasing scenario, full occupancy, and unrealistically low shoestring expenses.

The NOI calculation for a typical CRE property is shown in the table below.

Gross revenues
Plus: Other income (tenant reimbursements, parking, percentage rent, etc.)
Less: Vacancy
Equals: Effective gross income
Less: Operating expenses (excluding capital and tenant improvements and leasing commissions)
Equals: **Net operating income**

Let's review an example of a real acquisition transaction to show the contrasting NOIs for a 236,000-square-foot shopping center located in

Charleston, South Carolina, and placed up for sale earlier this year for $22 million. The property is a neighborhood shopping center in a B+ location, on twenty acres, 87 percent leased, and with major tenants Petco and Dollar Tree. The sales package from a national brokerage firm included the 2014 actual NOI and the 2015 pro-forma NOI of $1.325 million and $1.675 million, respectively. The purchaser's analysis of the deal produced his two different NOIs: an adjusted actual 2014 NOI of $1.275 million and a 2015 pro-forma NOI of $1.390 million. The purchaser's adjustments included higher vacancy for leases not signed, an increased management fee, and higher repair and maintenance expenses. These are typical adjustments made by purchasers during the deal-underwriting process. A table of the NOIs and cap rates follows:

	Seller		Purchaser	
	Actual 2014	Seller pro forma 2015	Purchaser adjusted 2014	Purchaser pro forma 2015
NOI	$1,325,000	$1,675,000	$1,275,000	$1,390,000
Asking/offering price	N/A	$22,000,000	N/A	$19,857,000
Capitalization rate	N/A	7.6%	N/A	7%

Based on the above data, the purchaser should use the pro-forma NOI of $1.390 million to determine his offer price for the property. If the purchaser's required capitalization rate is 7 percent, then the offer price for the property would be $19.857 million versus the seller's asking price of $22 million.

COMMANDMENT 16

Ten-year pro formas are worthless.

WHEN ACQUIRING CRE and during the due-diligence process, the buyer needs to underwrite the property. This usually entails preparation of an Excel spreadsheet (see commandment eleven on page 22) to determine the yearly net operating income, cash flow, and investment returns to both the sponsor of the investment and the equity investors. Most investors will calculate a free and clear internal rate of return on the net operating income and one based on the cash flow to the equity investors. The question for most investors is how many years into the future they should go with their underwriting spreadsheet. When I started in CRE in 1981 as a young controller and analyst at a major real estate syndicator, we prepared eleven-year pro formas. This included inflating out all the current leases, vacant space, and operating expenses over an eleven-year period. The primary underwriting term was ten years with the eleventh year used to calculate the terminal value of the property by capping out the eleventh-year net operating income at the purchase or going-in capitalization rate.

The problem with ten-year pro formas is that after the sixth or seventh year, these future income and expense figures are being established via an assumed inflation rate. The volatility of the economy and CRE industry has increased tremendously with shorter boom times and deeper and more devastating recessions. As mentioned previously, the holding period for CRE has shortened tremendously due to this dispersion. This volatility has made the ten-year pro forma almost worthless; I prefer a five- or maybe seven-year analysis when underwriting an investment and have found these time frames suitable for proper deal analysis.

COMMANDMENT 17

I have seldom seen the actual performance of a real estate investment agree to the acquisition pro forma.

THIS COMMANDMENT IS related to commandment sixteen on page 33 and refers to the inherent problem of trying to predict the future with financial models. Financial models are great to use, but many of us begin to rely on them as if they are always perfect and accurate. Even though financial underwriting and the models used are necessary, astute real estate investors know that real events will most likely be different. During my thirty-plus-year career in CRE, I have analyzed and underwritten hundreds of properties and portfolios and have rarely seen the actual performance of a property even remotely agree to the original underwriting pro forma. This is not the case with single-tenant net-lease deals, since they are fairly easy to underwrite with only one lease, but this commandment is more the rule than the exception when dealing with multitenant commercial properties and apartments.

What is the cause of this disparity in the projected amounts versus actual performance? It's always very difficult to predict future events, especially macro factors such as the economy, inflation, interest rates, and competition, and at the micro property level, predictability of the rental income is always challenging. The hardest portion of CRE underwriting is determining the effective gross income (EGI). EGI is the gross potential rent for all property spaces less vacancy plus other income such as tenant reimbursements, percentage rent, late fees, parking, and so on. Calculating future rents involves numerous assumptions in a variety of areas, such as current market rent, inflation expectations, probabilities of tenant renewals or exercising options, time frames for leasing of vacant spaces, overall building vacancy, estimates of other income from expense reimbursements, common-area maintenance payments, parking, late fees, and percentage rents. The difficulty in projecting future revenue and operating expenses makes it very difficult for the original underwriting pro forma to agree to actual events, and when it does, it's very rare and probably the result of blind luck.

Commandment 18

Do not commit funds to a real estate investment firm if none of the principals have gray hair and have not been through the last two secular downturns.

T HIS COMMANDMENT IS very important, especially for institutional investors. There are hundreds of CRE-investment funds sponsored by a variety of real estate private-equity firms, investment banks, commercial banks, sovereign-wealth funds, pension funds, and insurance companies. As of the writing of this book in spring 2015 and according to Preqin, an alternative asset-management data and research firm, there is more than $100 billion of real estate equity capital in commingled and separate account funds slated to be invested.

There are a variety of sponsors of these funds as listed above. Some are large and very well known, such as the Blackstone Group, Starwood Capital Group, and Colony Capital, and others consist of a few young people in office suites who are trying to close their first funds. I believe that the most important ingredient to being successful as a real estate private-equity firm is experience and knowledge of the firm's personnel. Senior-level individuals with the long-term tenure of being in the CRE industry for decades, the completing of numerous transactions throughout the country, and the painful experience of going through the two secular downturns of 1987–1992 and 2007–2012 have tremendous knowledge and understanding that equates to better investment decisions and performance. For example, I have personally seen numerous deals throughout the country on the market for sale and financing during the last dozen years that I was involved in acquiring or financing way back in the 1980s and 1990s. Since CRE is such a transaction-oriented business, the experience gained over many years is invaluable, and institutional investors should weigh the merits of committing funds to sponsors who do not have gray-haired, senior-level personnel.

COMMANDMENT 19

The skills and training of most on-site apartment-property managers are equivalent to those of the kids working at movie theaters.

APARTMENT PROPERTIES ARE the most management intensive of the four commercial property types (office buildings, shopping centers, apartments, and industrial warehouses), and there are many good management companies. However, having bought, financed, sold, and lived in dozens of apartment properties in Illinois, Texas, and California, I know that the skills and knowledge of a large number of on-site property managers are very deficient. The most critical operation for apartment ownership is the management function, and the most important person is the property manager.

Many apartment-management companies, whether they are owned by the owner of the property or a third-party management company, continue to hire inexperienced individuals at the property-manager level. This inexperience usually results in a poorly managed property with lower rents and cash flow and higher vacancy. The property managers do not in many cases have the requisite training, knowledge, and experience to excel at this function.

I am not dumping on the property manager but on the owner of the property or third-party management company who does not provide the experience and training for this key position. Additionally, property managers are not paid very well, with the salary of the head property manager at a midsize property of two hundred units at only $35,000 to $50,000 per year depending on the location. A good property manager who knows the intricacies of leasing, setting rental rates, maintenance issues, online tenant portals, repairs, staffing, customer or tenant service, and the local rental market is invaluable. An apartment property with a good versus an average or subpar property manager can generate a 5 percent to 10 percent higher net operating income. The problem in the property-management industry is that there are very few good managers and many poor managers, and the poor ones remind me of the young, inexperienced, and flaky high school kids who staff movie theaters.

COMMANDMENT 20

**If a mezzanine loan is not secured by the
property, then it's an equity investment.**

MEZZANINE LOANS ARE second, or in some cases third, mortgages on a property and as such are subordinate to the first mortgage. Prior to the Great Recession, most mezzanine loans were secured by a subordinate mortgage or deed of trust on the property that was governed by an intercreditor agreement between the mezzanine lender and holder of the first mortgage. The capital stack or capitalization for a typical $50 million transaction structured with mezzanine debt is included in the table below.

Capital Stack	Amount
First mortgage (70%)	$35,000,000
Mezzanine loan I (15%)	$7,500,000
Mezzanine loan II (10%)	$5,000,000
Owner equity (5%)	$2,500,000
Total capitalization (100%)	$50,000,000

During the Great Recession, many property owners defaulted on both the first mortgage and mezzanine debt, resulting in extensive litigation between these two parties about payment priorities, foreclosure, and other debt issues.

Today, most first-mortgage lenders are reluctant to allow a mezzanine lender to record a mortgage or deed of trust on the property in order to avoid these potential litigation issues. Since the mezzanine lender is not secured by the property, he or she typically receives as security for his or her investment a pledge of the owner's or sponsor's equity interest in the property and a personal guarantee. If the mezzanine lender does not have a recorded mortgage plus foreclosure and self-help rights in the event of a first-mortgage default, then this mezzanine capital is really an equity investment.

As an equity investment that may leverage up to 95 percent of the capitalization of the property, as shown above, the mezzanine lender is taking an equity-investment risk and therefore needs an equity-like return. One of the axioms of real estate and corporate finance is that debt is always cheaper than equity because it has priority over equity, it has to be paid back, and it is less risky; equity is always more expensive than debt because it doesn't have to be paid back and therefore is riskier. The $50 million property above is capitalized with a 70 percent first mortgage at $35 million, two mezzanine loans totaling $12.5 million, and owner equity of $2.5 million. The mezzanine lenders are taking 25 percent (the percentage amount of capital above the first mortgage and below the owner's investment) of the equity risk, and the internal rate or return on these loans should be around 15 percent. A return of 15 percent will provide the mezzanine lenders with an equity-type return commensurate with their level of risk. The mezzanine loan may be structured with the following terms: loan fees of 3 percent to 5 percent, interest rate of 10 percent with 6 percent paid and 4 percent accrued, and an equity participation of 15 percent in the cash flow and upon the occurrence of a liquidity event (i.e., sale or refinancing) of the property.

COMMANDMENT 21

**The more convoluted the capital stack, the
higher the odds the deal will tank.**

THE CAPITAL STACK on a CRE property refers to the multiple levels of debt
and equity financial investment in the asset with each level having its
own unique rights, protections, and financial returns. Prior to the financial
crash and the frenzy of deal making, the capital stacks on large institutional
properties become very unwieldy. The Stuyvesant Town–Peter Cooper Village
apartment complex discussed in commandment eight on page 16 is a prime
example. The capital stack for this deal included a securitized first mortgage
of $3 billion, five mezzanine-one loans totaling $300 million, two mezzanine-
two loans totaling $600 million, five mezzanine-three loans totaling $300
million, one final mezzanine loan of $200 million, and fifteen equity inves-
tors that invested $1.9 billion for a total capitalization of $6.3 billion.

The capital stack for CRE properties has evolved over time, depending on
the taxation policy, capital-market conditions, real estate financing innova-
tions, and risk tolerance. The table below shows the typical capital stack for
CRE over the last five decades.

1970s	1980s	1990s	2000s	2015
First mortgage loan at 70%	Wraparound mortgage loan at 85% that wraps around an underlying first mortgage at 70%	First mortgage loan at 70%	First mortgage securitized into CMBS (commercial mortgage-backed securities) at 70%	First mortgage at 65%
		Mezzanine loan at 20%	Mezzanine loans I & II at 20%	Owner equity investment at 35%
			Preferred equity investment at 5%	
Owner equity investment at 30%	Owner equity investment at 15%	Owner equity investment at 10%		
			Owner equity investment at 5%	

As shown in the table, the capital stack was very conservative in the 1970s, with a plain-vanilla mortgage provided by a bank or savings and loan and the owners' equity investment. In the 1980s, a common loan structure was a wraparound mortgage at high leverage. A wraparound mortgage is a subordinate loan that wraps around and encompasses the existing first mortgage so that the borrower only makes one debt payment to the wrap-loan mortgagee. These loans fell out of favor after the real estate crash and secular downturn from 1987 to 1992 and are not used anymore. The amount of leverage on a typical real estate property in the 1980s was very high, in the 80 percent to 95 percent range of the property value, due to the tax laws in that period that allowed the full deduction of all real estate losses and the promotion of CRE deals as tax shelters. After the real estate crash of the late eighties and early nineties, the capital stack again became conservative with a plain-vanilla 70 percent first mortgage and a 20 percent mezzanine loan and 10 percent equity.

The capital stack became very convoluted in the 2000s, primarily as the result of the Wall Street financial-engineering machine and easy money from lenders and investors. A typical property capitalization during this period included a 70 percent first mortgage that was securitized into commercial mortgage-backed securities; two mezzanine loans at 20 percent of the capital stack; preferred equity of 5 percent, which is an equity investor that has return preference over the owners' equity-investment group; and last and most certainly least, the 5 percent owners' equity investment. Today, the capital stack is back to being more conservative with a first mortgage at 65 percent and a large equity investment at 35 percent, with most of the equity emanating from pension funds, private real estate equity, institutional investors, or public investments through REITs.

The capital stack of CRE investments has evolved over time and depends on the capital markets, risk appetite, fiscal and monetary policy, and availability of credit. When the capital stack on a property becomes complex and unwieldy, that is a good indication that the deal will eventually tank.

COMMANDMENT 22

The more properties and portfolios an investor buys, the lower the quality of due diligence, which leads to poor performance in the future.

WHEN THE CRE business is booming, the acquisition machine of many investments firms is in overdrive. This occurred from 2004 through 2007 and in the current market in the spring of 2015. The larger the CRE-investment firm, the larger the deals its executives need to acquire to move the needle in their burgeoning portfolios. A CRE private-equity firm that owns $10 billion in assets will most likely not buy a $20 million property because it's too small, won't increase the overall fund return, and leaves them with much more idle funds to employ. Therefore, these large firms end up acquiring very large properties or asset portfolios in the core markets such as New York, Boston, Miami, San Francisco, Seattle, and Chicago.

A portfolio acquisition may consist of twenty, thirty, or even one hundred different properties that may be located across the country. The purchaser usually only has thirty to sixty days as required by the seller to perform due diligence on the portfolio, and therefore he or she ends up cutting corners or not completing a proper due-diligence review on each property in the portfolio. Sloppy due diligence may include not inspecting each property, not reviewing and abstracting all leases, not inspecting all vacant spaces, not receiving tenant-estoppel letters from all large tenants, and not completing thorough physical inspections of each property.

There is no excuse for not performing a comprehensive due-diligence review on a large portfolio of CRE assets. Even if the purchaser's due-diligence time is restricted, he or she still should have access to the appropriate number of personnel to complete the task. Inadequate due diligence for large and frequent portfolio acquisitions will inevitably lead to poor investment performance of the CRE assets in the future.

COMMANDMENT 23

In many acquisition deals, the bid-ask spread between the buyer and seller is usually equal to the brokerage fee.

THE CRE-ACQUISITION PROCESS typically involves the following steps:

+ A real estate broker is hired by the seller to market a property for a brokerage fee of 1 percent to 5 percent of the sales price. The higher the price of the property, the lower the percentage of the broker's fee. The asking price is usually set at a price that is 5 percent to 10 percent above the fair market value of the property.

+ The real estate broker prepares along with the seller a marketing package that is sent to qualified buyers.

+ Potential buyers review the package and perform a site visit to the property. If they are interested in the deal, they will send to the broker and seller a nonbinding letter of intent that expresses the buyer's terms to purchase the property.

+ The buyer's initial-offer purchase price will usually be 10 percent to 15 percent less than the seller's asking price.

+ The seller and buyer will negotiate a price, with the buyer increasing the original offer price and the seller reducing the original asking price, and execute an agreement of purchase and sale.

- ◆ Eventually, the buyer and seller will agree on a price or are very close on price, and the difference usually equals the brokerage fee.
- ◆ In many cases, a deal will be reached by asking the broker to reduce his or her fee to make the deal happen.

For example, an office building is marketed for sale at $20 million, and a potential buyer offers $17.75 million for the property. The seller counters the buyer's offer at $19 million. The buyer then increases his or her offer to $18.25 million. The seller considers the buyer's higher price and makes a final counteroffer of $18.75 million. The buyer now has three options: meet the seller's new asking price of $18.75 million, stay with his or her last offer of $18.25 million, or pass on the deal. If the buyer stays at $18.25 million, then the difference in price from the seller's latest asking price is $500,000, which just so happens to be close to the 2.5 percent brokerage fee on the deal.

In this situation, the brokerage firm will in many cases be asked to reduce its fee to make the deal happen. This will, however, depend on the size of the brokerage firm and its relationship with the seller. Most of the global real estate services firms with significant investment-sales operations will not reduce their fee, while smaller and local players will do so to close the transactions.

COMMANDMENT 24

**If you want to close real estate deals in an hour,
take all the chairs out of the conference room.**

THIS COMMANDMENT IS based on firsthand experience from the 1980s when
I was employed at a large financial-services and real estate firm that was
closing CRE acquisitions and loans on a monthly basis. The closings were usually at our office, and each one consistently took all day to close. Most of the
transactions were large and complicated real estate loans and acquisitions and
required all the parties to attend, including the borrower, seller (if an acquisition),
lawyers for all parties, real estate and mortgage brokers, and title-insurance company. Today, many closings are completed at the title-insurance company's office; however, some of the larger ones are at the lawyer's, seller's, or lender's office.

One method I discovered to reduce an all-day closing to an hour or so is
to take all the chairs out of the conference room. It's amazing to see how fast
a closing happens if everyone has to stand. At a closing, it is not the least bit
unusual to require last-minute changes to transaction documents. With no
chairs, the lawyers have to kneel down and make those changes while balanc-
ing on a conference table, and amazingly, the changes, agreements, and wire
transfers are finalized at warp speed. This commandment should also apply
to any personnel plagued by long and boring company meetings. Taking the
chairs out of the conference room will usually make the meetings short and
sweet.

COMMANDMENT 25

**You can't learn commercial real estate from a
book, video, or course; you have to do it.**

T HE CRE INDUSTRY is different from most other industries in that it is a
transaction-oriented business. This means that the industry is based on
the volume of leasing, financing, and sales transactions. Fewer CRE transactions equate to reduced income for those working in the CRE industry. In
times of plenty, everyone reaps the financial benefits from the high volume
of transactions. If there are few or no transactions, many in the industry will
earn very little money. There are also many different disciplines in the CRE
industry that share in the fees or payments when transaction volume is high.
These different disciplines typically include the following:

- The lenders who make the loan
- The real estate brokers who market the property for sale or negotiate
  the tenant lease
- The lawyers who work on behalf of the each party in the transaction
- The title company that provides the lender and property-title insurance
- The appraisal firm that provides an appraisal to the buyer and lender
- The engineering firm that completes the physical inspection of the
  property

- The accounting firm that assists with the due diligence and provides accounting, auditing, and tax services for the property and owner
- The environmental firm that completes the Phase I or II environmental review of the property
- The investment advisors and placement agents that arrange the equity investment in the property
- The mortgage brokers who arrange the financing on the property
- The surveying firm that completes a survey of the property

To learn the CRE business, one must usually start at the bottom as an analyst or junior broker and absorb the business by being involved in numerous transactions over years and decades. This transaction experience provides participants with a wealth of information, knowledge, and experience about property types, leases, deal structures, financing, capital markets, development, investment strategies, financial metrics, management, and operations. CRE knowledge and experience cannot be gained from reading a book, watching a video, or taking a course, even though these are worthwhile endeavors. To become a successful real estate executive, an individual must obtain experience in the industry by doing multiple transactions over a long period of time.

COMMANDMENT 26

Commercial real estate investment is a very inefficient business; however, the competition for deals is intense.

THE CRE BUSINESS, as was previously stated, is a transaction-oriented business based on leases, financings, and sales. The total value of CRE debt and equity investment in the United States is approximately $5 trillion. The CRE-investment process is very inefficient, as each property, location, lease structure, market, and investment strategy is different. Every real estate property has unique characteristics due to the location, building design, type of lease, age of the property, market area, and local demographics. Lease terms are also different depending on the type of property and location. For example, office lease terms are different in New York versus San Francisco versus Dallas. Much of the property-level and lease data is also not made public, which adds to the industry inefficiency.

The local real estate market in which each property is located has its own unique characteristics due to the demographics, weather, industry concentration, and competitive properties. The investment strategy of each CRE investor is also unique and may be based on buying institutional-quality core assets in large cities such as New York, Boston, and San Francisco or acquiring retail properties that need significant renovation, tenant realignment, and leasing. All of these divergent characteristics of the CRE industry make it a very inefficient business model. In addition, CRE is a hard asset with primarily long-term leases, which contributes to its inefficient nature. Although the CRE market is generally inefficient, the competition for deals is fierce. This is mainly the result of the capital markets. If capital is cheap, as it is today, with zero short-term interest rates, then investment activity will be high, as CRE buyers have easy access to debt and equity capital to make investments.

Today, any large, institutional-quality CRE property that is placed on the market for sale in a core market such as New York or San Francisco will get twenty to thirty bids. The same would be the case for a suburban garden-apartment building located in a suburb of Dallas. Even though the CRE business model is inefficient, there is intense competition for investments, especially when the capital markets are friendly.

COMMANDMENT 27

The seller always knows more about his or her property than the buyer does.

COMMANDMENT TWENTY-THREE ON page 48 outlined the general steps involved in acquiring a CRE asset. During this process, the purchaser will review the seller's sales package and, if interested in the property, will make the seller an offer. If the offer is accepted, the parties will proceed to close the acquisition. Prior to closing the acquisition, the purchaser will perform a detailed due-diligence review of the property, including an engineering, financial, and physical review. Although the purchaser performs this comprehensive due diligence, the purchaser will never know as much about the property in question as the seller.

The seller always knows more about his or her property than a potential purchaser does, and this is obviously because the seller has owned the property for a period of time and knows all the intricacies of the asset, from which tenants pay their rent slowly to which roofs leak to information about the proposed development of a competing building down the street. Even though the purchaser performs this comprehensive and detailed due-diligence review, he or she will never know more about the property than the seller does.

COMMANDMENT 28

The most successful commercial real estate investors have a long-term time horizon.

A CRE ASSET CAN be broken down into a hard asset or building located on a parcel of land and occupied by a cluster of tenants with leases. The tenants' lease payments (rent) generate income that is used to pay expenses of operating the building with amounts left over being used first to pay any debt on the property and last to be distributed to the owner and investors of the property. The value of a CRE asset is therefore derived from the leases—which provide an income stream—and, over time, from higher rents. As the rents increase, so will the value of the property; however, this may take years depending on the local market, economy, interest rates, management, competition, and other property-related factors. Two benefits of holding CRE long-term are the equity accumulated from debt amortization and deferred payment of capital-gain taxes. If a property is financed with an amortizing mortgage, each mortgage payment gradually but steadily reduces the principal balance of the mortgage, thereby increasing the equity in the property. Property held long-term is not subject to capital-gain taxes until sold, which also benefits the property owner. Long-term owners of property can also take cash out of the property through debt refinancing. The net proceeds of the refinanced debt can be distributed to the investors, which is typically a nontaxable transaction; however, taxability may depend on the investor's basis in the partnership or other ownership-entity structure.

Since the value of CRE is based on increasing rents, the longer a property is held, the higher its value. However, as discussed in commandment thirteen, the volatility of the industry has gotten much worse, as the growth periods have become shorter and the contraction cycles have grown longer and more severe. Due to this volatility, the holding period for CRE assets has declined to an average of about three years. In essence, a large part of the CRE industry has become a trading market, and the dominant strategy is now similar to a market-timing strategy when acquiring corporate-equity securities. Big profits can be earned from short-term trading of CRE, and this typically occurs by buying at discounted values during severe downturns and reselling when the economy recovers. However, this subjects the seller to capital-gain taxes and transaction fees. The most successful CRE investors do have long-term holding periods, and the best evidence of this are the New York real estate families such as the Dursts, Trumps, LeFraks, Rudins, and others. These families, many of whom are billionaires, are long-term owners and developers of real estate property and rarely sell their assets.

COMMANDMENT 29

If the seller and broker tell you, the purchaser, that once you buy the property, you will be able to raise the rents and increase occupancy and net operating income significantly, ask them, "Why haven't you done it?"

D URING MY CAREER, I have been involved in more than $1.5 billion of CRE-acquisition transactions across the spectrum of property types and around the country. One comment I have often heard from the seller or broker when acquiring CRE is, "The property is only eighty-eight percent leased, but when you buy it, you will be able to increase the occupancy at good rents and increase the net operating income well above our pro-forma amount." This comment typically is made when acquiring property that is underperforming, has high vacancy, is in need of significant renovation, or has other negative attributes. In these situations, the seller and broker want the buyer to become emotionally engaged with the thought of quick profits and overpay for the property, as if it's fully leased with superior-credit tenants and above-market financial performance. Regardless of the cause of the current underperformance—poor management, unpredictable tenancy changes, or something else—the seller wants the new buyer to overlook these negatives and pay a premium for the property based on these future speculations.

Whenever I hear these sales pitches, I laugh and ask the seller and broker, "If it's that simple, why don't you do it?" If I as the naïve buyer can raise the rents, lower the vacancy, and increase the net operating income once I own the property and potentially create millions of dollars in value, then why doesn't the seller do it and earn this additional value increase?

COMMANDMENT 30

I have rarely seen a lender collect on a personal loan guarantee.

MOST PERMANENT REAL estate mortgages on property having market or above-market occupancy rates are nonrecourse except for "bad boy" carve-outs, such as a bankruptcy filing, fraud, or theft. Nonrecourse means that the lender can look to only the real estate asset and not the personal assets of the owners as repayment of the loan. It's typically a bit different for real estate construction loans and those made by small banks to operator-owners at the local real estate level, which are usually full recourse. A full-recourse loan is one in which the lender has a mortgage on the property and a guarantee of the loan repayment secured by the personal assets of the owner or sponsor of the property. A full-recourse loan is evidenced by a separate guarantee agreement signed by the principal of the borrower. The guarantee agreement typically provides that the borrower is personally liable for repayment of the real estate loan in full, and should there be a default and foreclosure, the borrower's personal assets would be utilized to fund any deficiency.

During my career, I have originated, negotiated, funded, and analyzed more than $1 billion in CRE loans of all types of properties located throughout the country. Many of these loans were construction loans for the development of new properties, which, being risky transactions, almost always required the borrower to personally guarantee the loans. Even with this extra layer of protection, in the event of default, it is rare that lenders pursue these personal assets—and rarer for a lender to collect on the personal guarantee. The reasons are the time and expense it takes in litigation to obtain a judgment against the borrowers/guarantors; the possibility that guarantors may file bankruptcy, making it difficult to collect on the debt; and the chance that borrowers may, through trusts, offshore entities, and other schemes, shield their assets from the lender.

COMMANDMENT 31

**Never buy or capitalize a property if the mortgage
rate is greater than the capitalization rate.**

T HE MOST IMPORTANT metric in acquiring or valuing CRE is the capitalization rate (see commandment one on page 1). The capitalization rate is
the property's net operating income (the cash revenues less noncapitalized operating expenses) divided by the property purchase price or value. The higher
the capitalization rate, the better the investment. The acquisition of a CRE
property typically includes a debt component secured by a lender's first mortgage on the property and an equity-investment component provided by the
owners or investors.

For example, ACME Property Company is buying a $10 million office
building with a net operating income of $800,000. In other words, the prop-
erty is being purchased for an 8 percent capitalization rate. ACME will finance the acquisition of the building with a new first mortgage at 75 percent
of value or $7.5 million and an equity investment of $2.5 million. The mortgage loan has an interest rate of 6.5 percent, a thirty-year amortization, and an
annual payment of $568,861. The cash flow after debt service and the return
on equity are shown in the table below:

ACME office building	Amount
Net operating income	$800,000
Debt service (principal and interest)	$568,861
Cash flow to the equity investors	$231,139
Equity investment	$2,500,000
Cash flow return on equity	9.2%

As shown in this table, ACME has a return on equity of 9.2 percent. This is because the capitalization rate on the property of 8 percent is higher than the mortgage rate of 6.5 percent and produces positive leverage. Positive leverage occurs when either the interest rate on the debt is less than the capitalization rate or the cost of debt capital is less than the discount rate return on the property. Investors should never buy or capitalize a property wherein the interest rate on the debt is higher than the capitalization rate on the property. This is known as negative leverage. If ACME had purchased the property at a 6 percent instead of the 8 percent capitalization rate, the return on investor equity would only be 1.2 percent. Therefore, positive leverage enhances the return on equity while negative leverage reduces the return on equity.

COMMANDMENT 32

The higher the capitalization rate on a property, the greater the ability of the property to absorb the various risks inherent in commercial real estate.

ONE OF THE iconic stock investors of the twentieth century was the great Benjamin Graham. Mr. Graham was a deep-value investor (i.e., seeking good companies selling at a significant discount), and one of his most important metrics was what he called "the margin of safety." The margin of safety according to Graham is the difference between a stock's price and its intrinsic or discounted cash-flow value. Graham looked to buy stocks for which the market price of the stock was at least 50 percent of the intrinsic price of the company. In this situation, Graham was buying that stock at a 50 percent discount to intrinsic value, which provided a buffer or cushion in case something went wrong with the company or the calculation of the perceived intrinsic value was incorrect or faulty.

The same scenario applies to the CRE industry and capitalization rates. The capitalization rate, as discussed in commandment one on page 1, is the net operating income from the property divided by the property's price or value. The higher the capitalization rate, the higher the cash flow before debt on the property, and the better the property will be able to absorb any negative factors affecting it. These negative factors may include lower rents, higher expenses, higher vacancy, loss or bankruptcy of a major tenant, adverse changes in the market or economy, higher-interest rates, or other risks of owning commercial real estate. See commandment forty-four on page 88 for a more thorough discussion of the fifteen risks inherent in CRE investment.

COMMANDMENT 33

**Location, occupancy, and quality of the property are
great, but cash flow is king in commercial real estate.**

T HIS COMMANDMENT IS one of the keys to success in CRE investment and
means that the most important financial metric of a property is the capitalization rate or how much cash flow before debt the property throws off. All
other metrics of a real estate property such as location, occupancy, tenancy,
quality of the property, and financial structure are important, but cash flow is
king. Cash flow from a CRE property is the income derived from the tenant
leases less the operating expenses. Net cash flow is the net operating income
less debt service. The higher the occupancy and lease rates and the lower the
property expenses, the higher the cash flow. Also, the lower and more favorable the interest rate on the property debt, the higher the cash flow.

Owning a class-C property that throws off a lot of cash flow is superior to
owning a brand-new property that has high vacancy or a poor rent structure.
It is better to own a dilapidated, 100 percent leased shopping center in a low-
income market with average rents but high sales volumes that throws off a lot
of cash than to own a 90 percent leased, high-end-lifestyle shopping center
that is located in a wealthy area but leaves only minimal funds in your wallet
after all the bills are paid.

COMMANDMENT 34

If you are a commercial real estate syndicator buying numerous deals per year, you are not in the commercial real estate business; you are a marketing organization.

REAL ESTATE SYNDICATORS are investment firms that acquire numerous properties per year and raise capital for each deal separately or in a fund format structured as a limited partnership, limited liability company, or private real estate investment trust. These syndicators need to constantly raise large amounts of capital to fund their real estate acquisition machine, and over time, the emphasis is on raising capital more than a didactic investigation of the metrics of the individual commercial real estate property. Many of these syndicators acquired tenants in common properties prior to the Great Recession. These were properties that included up to thirty-five individual equity investors that provided equity capital in a tax-free exchange to the syndicator to acquire the property. To most of these syndicators, selling and marketing the investor capital becomes more important than buying and managing the actual real estate property. This is because they need the fees generated from each syndication to fund the burgeoning overhead costs of their business. Without these fees, many syndicators would not be able to financially support their organizations.

The structure of these syndication deals usually includes a front-end load of 10 percent to 13 percent of the equity capital raised. The largest portion of the front-end load goes to paying a 7 percent commission to the financial advisor, registered investment advisor, or broker selling the deal and 1 percent to his firm as a dealer manager fee or override fee. The sponsor of the fund will receive 3 percent to 5 percent of the total load for various fees, including the acquisition fee, financing fee, deal-monitoring fee, management fee, and organization fee. The total selling fee of 8 percent is the largest portion of the front-end load and additional evidence that these companies are more marketing organizations than real estate investment firms.

COMMANDMENT 35

The most important metric for retail real estate after the capitalization rate is the sales volume per square foot of the anchor tenants.

S HOPPING-CENTER INVESTMENTS ARE the most difficult CRE projects to acquire, own, and manage due to the intricacies of retail leases and competition in the sector. Retail leases are the most complex in CRE due to the following typical provisions:

- Cotenancy clause: clause that allows a tenant to terminate his or her lease or reduce his or her rent if occupancy declines below a specific amount and/or certain tenants (usually the anchors) cease doing business in the shopping center
- Percentage rent: additional rent based on a negotiated percentage of the tenant's sales in excess of a base amount
- CAM costs: common-area maintenance costs that the tenant reimburses to the landlord
- Tenant improvements: who pays for and owns the improvement made to the tenant's space
- Assignment and subleasing rights: rights required by the tenant to assign or sublease his or her space, usually only with approval by the landlord

- ◆ Subordination and nondisturbance agreement: this requires that the lease is subordinate to any financing on the property, and if the lender forecloses on the property, it will not disturb the tenant's leasehold interest in the property

When acquiring retail properties, the second most important metric after the capitalization rate is the sales volume of the anchor tenants. This is critical data because it indicates how well the tenant(s) are operating in that location. Retail leases should require that at least the anchor tenants provide the landlord with quarterly sales data. Tenant leases that contain a percentage rent clause as mentioned above will require sales data as the basis for the calculation of the percentage rent.

A tenant with a high sales volume per square foot indicates that the tenant is in a great location and real estate and consumer market. It will usually be difficult for retail competitors to enter that market and capture some of the tenant's high sales volume. This is because there may not be a competing shopping center with adequate space for the competitor or the market is not big enough to support two similar retailers in the market. This is like having a so-called moat around the shopping center, a term Warren Buffett uses when he buys companies. When a company has a moat around it, that moat protects the company's products, sales, and business from competition.

The sales volume per square foot depends on the type of retailer and the size of his or her space. Department stores will have lower sales volume per square foot than jewelry stores do because the latter are much smaller and sell higher-margin merchandise. Sales volumes will also vary depending on how well the retailer is managed and if the company is in financial distress. For example, Macy's, a growing and successful large department-store chain, has an average sales volume of about $500 per square foot, while Sears, a struggling department-store chain has sales per square foot of only about $150 per square foot. The highest sales volume retailers are Apple at about $6,000 per square foot and Tiffany & Co. at about $3,000 per square foot. The higher the sales volume for retail tenants in a shopping center, the better the real estate property.

Commandment 36

Vertically integrated real estate developers have a competitive advantage in a bull market but will be at extreme risk in a recessionary environment.

VERTICAL INTEGRATION IS defined as the process in which several steps in the production and/or distribution of a product or service are controlled by a single business entity in an effort to increase that entity's power in the marketplace. In CRE, a vertically integrated developer is one in which a holding or development company possesses the key functions to develop CRE within separate groups or divisions. This could include an internal land acquisition and entitlement group, general contractor, project-management group, brokerage team, and development and property-management business units. This type of business model allows the developer to integrate and control all aspects of the CRE-development process from land acquisition to property management to divestiture. During boom times when land, tenants, and capital are readily available, this model will perform very well, as each group under the holding-company umbrella operates efficiently and seamlessly across a multitude of land acquisitions, development projects, and other transactions. The development company reaps hefty fees self-performing each of these functions and realizes strong capital appreciation of its development portfolio.

Vertical integration is a big handicap for a development company when the economy turns down or is in a recession or interest rates begin to rise. In a shrinking market, the development company is typically left holding vacant warehoused land with no income, new construction has come to a standstill, the operating income from its owned properties is in decline, and fee generation deteriorates. This reduction in business and fees will reduce the development company's cash flow and make it very difficult, if not impossible, to carry or fund its various groups and divisions. If the downturn is severe and lasts long enough, the development company will likely suffer layoffs and possible dissolution or elimination of a number of its development divisions to conserve cash and keep the parent company solvent. A vertically integrated CRE-development firm will perform well in a booming economy and real estate market but will incur extensive losses and may be close to bankruptcy in a down market or recession.

COMMANDMENT 37

**Borrowing short and investing long is one of the
riskiest strategies in the commercial real estate industry
and is the cause of most financial crashes.**

M OST FINANCIAL PANICS or crashes in the CRE industry are caused by
investors and lenders that borrow short and invest long. This was a primary driver of the bankruptcy of Lehman Brothers and Bear Stearns investment banks in 2008. These firms relied on short-term repurchase-agreement loans to fund their operations and invested that capital in long-term investments in real estate, private equity, hedge funds, and other alternative assets. This was also the downfall of many investment firms, mortgage REITs, and shadow financial firms during the Great Recession.

When CRE and financial firms borrow on a short-term basis and invest on a long-term basis, this creates a mismatch of assets and liabilities on the balance sheet. This may be fine when the economy is growing and the financial markets are stable. However, it is a death sentence when the economy contracts and credit becomes tight. As the credit market tightens, interest rates rise, and firms that borrow short see the cost of their liabilities increase. While the cost of their liabilities is increasing, the returns on their assets are primarily fixed because they are long-term investments. These long-term investments may also be difficult to sell, even at discounted values, and the firm may suffer liquidity risk by not being able to sell investments to pay off its short-term liabilities.

Due to the Federal Reserve's current zero-interest-rate policy, the cost of short-term floating-rate debt with interest rates correlated to LIBOR (London interbank offered rate) is very cheap. Six-month LIBOR is currently seventy-four basis points (1 percent is equal to 100 basis points), and the one-year rate is forty-three basis points. Many established CRE-investment firms today are borrowing at one-year LIBOR plus a spread of about 2 percent or a total floating rate of 2.74 percent. This is very cheap capital and one reason that property prices in many markets are in bubble territory. Even if the interest rate is swapped for a fixed rate, the term is typically short at only about one year. Using one-year debt to buy a long-term asset such as CRE is very dangerous and is one of the riskiest strategies in the business. The risk is that the economy will turn down, interest rates will rise or credit markets will tighten, and the property owner will have to refinance the short-term debt at a higher rate just when the cash flow and value of the property softens. The investor may also be unable to roll over or refinance the LIBOR loan, similar to what happened to many firms in the Great Recession, which led to project defaults and foreclosures. Borrowing short and investing long in CRE is a very risky strategy and should be avoided at all costs.

COMMANDMENT 38

Hotels are 70 percent operating business and 30 percent real estate investment. Senior-housing facilities (depending on type: independent living, assisted living, or nursing facility) are 80 percent to 95 percent operating business and 5 percent to 20 percent real estate investment. Therefore, good management and operations are the keys to success with these types of properties.

I N ADDITION TO the four basic property types in commercial real estate—multifamily apartments, office buildings, shopping centers, and industrial warehouses—there are two other property sectors that are important investment alternatives. They are hotels and senior housing. Both of these property sectors have distinctive investment, operational, and management properties that are keys to their success.

The hotel sector is made up of different brands or market segmentation related to the levels of services and amenities provided. These include budget, limited service, extended stay, luxury, boutique, and resort. Although the real estate components (location, design, physical plant, and so on) of a hotel are important to its success, the operations and management functions are an even more critical component, as hotel operations require a focus on sound business fundamentals and exceptional customer service. There are many employees working in a hotel, including desk staff, housekeeping staff, maintenance staff, garage attendants, bellhops, food and beverage workers, and so on. Hotels are also subject to management and franchise agreements. Management agreements provide for a hotel-management company to control the day-to-day operations of the hotel. Typical management fees are 2 percent to 4 percent of gross revenue plus an incentive fee that can reach 10 percent to 20 percent of cash flow after debt service. The most recognizable hotels, such as Hyatt, Hilton, Sheraton, Marriott, Radisson, and others, are franchises and are operated pursuant to a franchise agreement with the corporate parent company.

In a franchise arrangement, the hotel owner acquires a license from the hotel company to operate the hotel with the corporate brand name. The franchise also provides access to the brand's marketing muscle and reservations network, greater operational control through self-management or management by an independent operator, and facilitation of debt and equity financing (many lenders will not finance hotel construction or acquisition unless the property has a strong national brand). Other hotel companies, such as Best Western, have a membership association that requires hotels that label themselves as a Best Western to provide certain services, amenities, and property design to be a member and charge a membership fee that is typically less than a franchise fee. The membership fee is usually a fixed amount plus a variable amount per room, paid monthly or quarterly.

I consider hotels to be 70 percent business operation and 30 percent real estate investment. Although the real estate attributes, such as physical plant, location, age, amenities, and so on, are important, the real value is generated by the management and operational functions. The successful operation and increase in value of a hotel asset is therefore dependent on the management of the property, employees, and hotel profit centers—such as restaurants, spas, valet parking, business meetings, and events—and obtaining the property franchise and brand. The most successful hotel companies are the ones with the best management and operational capabilities.

Similar to hotels, senior-housing properties have real estate components such as location, physical plant, and design. However, due to the high level of care and medical requirements provided to the residents or patients, senior-housing properties are even more dependent on management and operations than hotels are, and the key to their value enhancement is the management of the facility and the quality of care provided to the residents and patients. Independent-living facilities are basically apartments for seniors who are typically eighty years old and older. I consider these projects to be 80 percent operating business and 20 percent real estate investment. Assisted-living facilities provide daily care to residents who need some assistance related to bathing, eating, medicine, or dementia. These facilities are 90 percent operating business and 10 percent real estate. Skilled-nursing facilities provide daily continuing care to patients who are chronically ill, have a higher level of medical acuity, require assistance with daily living, and are in need of rehabilitation services. Nursing facilities are 95 percent operating business and 5 percent real estate investment.

Both of these types of investments, hotels and senior housing, are primarily operating businesses more than real estate investments and need to be operated and managed as such. During my career, I've seen many real estate developers or investors acquire hotels and senior-housing properties without the requisite knowledge and experience in managing and operating these businesses. In most cases, these investments turned out to be unprofitable or were losing enterprises due to this lack of management and operation experience. Hotels and senior housing can be great investments; however, since they are operating businesses, they are higher-risk enterprises and therefore sell at higher cap rates than the four primary property types.

COMMANDMENT 39

Underwriting a commercial real estate deal with the terminal capitalization rate lower than the going-in capitalization rate means the deal doesn't work.

THE PROCESS FOR underwriting a new CRE acquisition is to prepare a five-, seven-, or ten-year (see commandment sixteen on page 33) pro forma and a terminal value/disposition valuation and discount these amounts at the acquiring real estate firms weighted-average cost of capital or discount rate. One of the key components of the discounting process is to calculate the terminal value, or the value of the property in the future, at the end of the analysis period. This is done by taking the net operating income from the year subsequent to the analysis period and applying a capitalization rate to that net operating income to calculate the terminal value.

Most CRE investors use the same capitalization rate to determine the terminal value as the one used to acquire the property, or the going-in capitalization rate. For example, if the going-in capitalization rate is 7 percent and the analysis period is five years, then the terminal value would be calculated by using the sixth-year net operating income and dividing it by the 7 percent capitalization rate.

Investors who use a lower capitalization rate to determine the terminal value do so primarily to increase the investor return and make the deal "work." This is a very risky underwriting strategy and should be avoided.

Manipulating the underwriting pro forma to obtain the desired return means the price paid for the property is too high, and the property investment should be rejected. Most real estate investment firms apply conservative underwriting principles by using the same terminal capitalization as the going-in rate to calculate the terminal value. Some firms use a higher terminal-value capitalization rate because of the increased aging of the property and required future capital improvements.

COMMANDMENT 40

The REIT structure is great for owning commercial real estate assets; however, REITs are required to pay out most of their cash flow. Therefore, internal growth is minimal, and they must grow externally via acquisition.

REAL ESTATE INVESTMENT trusts are income-tax-created entities that must hold real estate assets or mortgages pursuant to the following general regulations:

- Be an entity that would be taxable as a corporation but for its REIT status
- Be managed by a board of directors or trustees
- Have a minimum of one hundred shareholders after the first year as a REIT
- Have no more than 50 percent of the shares held by five or fewer individuals during the last half of the taxable year
- Invest at least 75 percent of the total assets in real estate assets and cash
- Derive at least 75 percent of the gross income from real estate sources, including rents from real property and interest on mortgages financing real property
- Derive at least 95 percent of the gross income from real estate and mortgage sources and dividends or interest from any source

- Have no more than 25 percent of the assets consist of nonqualifying securities or stock in taxable REIT subsidiaries
- Be required to pay out 90 percent of their taxable income as dividends to be exempt from paying income tax

REITs were formed in the 1960s as a way for individual investors to invest in commercial real estate companies and the like. They were created to be passive investment vehicles, similar to mutual funds, and if they pay out 90 percent of their taxable income as dividends, they are not subject to income tax. The 90 percent payout requirement usually requires most REITs to pay out a high percentage of their cash flow after debt, and therefore they do not generate sufficient internal net cash flow to grow. Additionally, the real estate assets of the four primary property types are usually encumbered with long-term leases that provide for very small annual rent increases of usually 2 percent to 4 percent. The payout ratio of a high percentage of a REIT's cash flow as dividends and long-term leases are characteristics of REITs that do not allow for high levels of internal growth. A corporate operating company (a company that makes or sells a product or service other than CRE) making widgets does not have these restrictions and therefore can grow very fast internally with sales and volume increases.

To grow their net operating income, funds from operations, FFO (net income plus depreciation and amortization excluding any gains and losses), dividends, and business, in general, REITs must grow via acquisition. A successful REIT business model is based on increasing the net operating income of internally owned properties and growing externally by acquiring or developing property. The stock price of a REIT may increase without external growth by either capitalization-rate compression (the capitalization rate applied to the REIT's net operating income decreases) or FFO multiple expansion. This is what has been occurring during the last few years under the Federal Reserve's zero-interest-rate policy program. The most successful and highest growth REITs have business models that include growing the net operating income of owned properties and acquiring or developing new properties.

COMMANDMENT 41

Beware of the real estate markets in Atlanta, Austin, Charlotte, Dallas, Denver, Houston, Phoenix, Tampa, , and Las Vegas. These cities and markets have a lot of vacant land and few development controls and are therefore high-beta markets with high volatility of real estate asset values and pricing.

THE CRE MARKETS in the cities of, Atlanta, Austin, Charlotte, Dallas, Denver, Houston, Phoenix, Tampa, and Las Vegas are very robust, as they and their metropolitan statistical areas are growing very fast with high migration of people and businesses. These markets also have a lot of available land and very few development controls, and so I call them high-beta markets. Beta is an investment term that relates the price change in a common stock to a broad or market-wide index such as the S&P 500 and is a measure of stock-volatility risk. A stock with a beta of 1.5 will move 1.5 times the S&P 500 index. If the index goes up 10 percent, the stock will go up 15 percent, and if the index drops 10 percent, the stock will drop 15 percent. The higher the beta, the more volatile the stock.

The CRE industry in these high-beta markets exhibits high volatility characterized by excessive boom and bust periods. This scenario is due to their prodevelopment policies and the large amount of vacant and developable land in these markets. When times are booming with a strong economy and favorable capital markets, they exhibit a high level of development activity that usually leads to overbuilding in almost all property types. Currently, most of the high-beta markets are overbuilt in apartments. According to Integra Realty Resources, an appraisal and feasibility firm, these high-beta markets have more than 102,000 apartment units under construction/completion in 2015, which is almost one-third of the total to be completed throughout the country.

The overbuilding in these high-beta markets leads to high vacancies, lower rents, higher capitalization rates, and properties in distress. Investors who develop or acquire CRE assets in these high-beta markets must be cognizant of the volatility in these areas and adjust their investment strategy accordingly.

COMMANDMENT 42

A portfolio acquisition of commercial real estate properties is comprised of "pigs and queens." There are a few queens and a lot of pigs, and the rest are in between. Therefore, the buyer needs a Kmart discount on a portfolio acquisition.

THE ACQUISITION OF portfolios of CRE properties is common in the industry. These portfolios may consist of a singular property type such as apartments or net-lease deals, properties based in a specific geographical region (e.g., two thousand apartment units in the southwestern United States), or mixed portfolios that include one or more of the four primary property types. The typical buyers of portfolios are the large real estate private-equity firms, REITs, and other institutional investors who have billions of assets under management and need large portfolios to realize any meaningful growth.

Usually, larger portfolios of at least ten or more properties are comprised of a few quality or class-A deals, the *queens*; many low-quality or class-C deals, the *pigs*; and a balance of class-B medium-quality deals. One of the potential benefits of acquiring a portfolio is that the buyer should get the proverbial Kmart discount via a higher capitalization rate of 0.5 percent to 1.5 percent due to its ability to take down the entire portfolio, the higher risk from the hodgepodge of property types, disparate locations, and management inefficiencies.

From the sellers perspective, large portfolios are a way of getting rid of the pigs in their portfolios in one fell swoop. However, many of these sellers also believe that they will get the same pricing and capitalization rate that is prevalent on the quality deals in the portfolio. Astute buyers know this and will negotiate a lower price to account for the pigs in the portfolio. They will seek the Kmart discount on the entire portfolio. In very large portfolios, some institutional buyers will immediately sell or flip many of the lower-quality properties in smaller or sub-portfolios and keep the higher-quality queens.

COMMANDMENT 43

Many suburban office buildings that have high vacancy will never achieve a stabilized 95 percent occupancy and, when acquired, should be underwritten at an 80 percent, 85 percent, or 90 percent occupancy level.

MANY SUBURBAN OFFICE buildings today are not fully leased. This has primarily been due to the slow growth of the white-collar workforce since the early 1990s, the Great Recession of 2007 to 2012, the lower rate of new-business formation, and muted job growth during and after this period. When acquiring suburban office buildings that are only 80 percent or so leased, potential buyers risk severely overpaying for a property then should they underwrite the acquisition at a 95 percent occupancy level. Many unsophisticated buyers will do this believing that they will be able to get the project fully leased even though the average occupancy during the last fifteen years has hovered in the mid- to high eighties. The seller will also assume that the property will get to 95 percent occupancy in a year or two, even though during the time he or she owned and managed it, the occupancy never exceeded 85 percent. The seller will do this by showing in the marketing and sales package the vacant space leased at the market rent on the rent roll and in the pro-forma cash flow. The seller believes that the buyer will base his or her purchase price on this inflated net operating income.

The more astute buyers will know that the underwritten vacancy is too low, and their Excel spreadsheet will include a market-based occupancy at 85 percent or 90 percent and an offer price based on these amounts. This offer price will usually be substantially below the seller's asking price, as the seller based his or her price on the higher occupancy level as discussed above. Purchasers must be aware of this vacancy issue with suburban buildings and not overpay for these assets.

COMMANDMENT 44

Many investors are not aware of the multitude of risks inherent in commercial real estate investment.

I HAVE IDENTIFIED FIFTEEN key risks in CRE investment. Most real estate firms do not focus on strategies to reduce or mitigate these risks. The risks are as follows:

1. Cash-flow risk: volatility in the property's net operating income or cash flow
2. Property-value risk: a reduction in a property's value
3. Tenant risk: loss or bankruptcy of a major tenant
4. Market risk: negative changes in the local real estate market or metropolitan statistical area
5. Economic risk: negative changes in the macro economy
6. Interest-rate risk: an increase in interest rates
7. Inflation risk: an increase in inflation
8. Leasing risk: inability to lease vacant space or a drop in lease rates
9. Management risk: poor management policy and operations
10. Ownership risk: loss of critical personnel of owner or sponsor
11. Legal and title risk: adverse legal issues and claims on title
12. Construction risk: development delays, cessation of construction, financial distress of general contractor or subcontractors, and payment defaults

13. Entitlement risk: inability or delay in obtaining project entitlements
14. Liquidity risk: inability to sell property or convert equity value into cash
15. Refinancing risk: inability to refinance property

The above list is not all-inclusive but represents key risk areas for any CRE owner. The list does not include geographic, property type, and industry concentration risks that should be considered at the asset allocation level in the CRE-investment process and are discussed in commandment four on page 7. Every CRE owner should be cognizant of the risks of owning CRE and the potential effects these risks have on the performance and value of the real estate assets.

All investors who own CRE should perform a detailed and systematic review of the above risks and their potential effect on an asset or portfolio. An easy way to perform this review is to assign points to each property based on one of three risk levels that correspond to each of the fifteen risks. For example, zero points can be assigned for no risk, one point for moderate risk, and two points for high risk. If the property is subject to all fifteen risks and the rating is zero to ten points, there is minimal risk; eleven to twenty points, there is moderate risk; and twenty-one points and over is high risk. The cumulative risk rating for the property can then be calculated. Once the risk factor is known, ownership can take the necessary steps to mitigate or eliminate these risks.

A CRE owner should perform, at least annually, the above risk assessment of his or her portfolio or property. In practice, this is rarely done and one of the main reasons for subpar investment performance and returns. Implementing this analytical framework to access risks inherent in CRE and then taking steps to minimize or eliminate these risks is a proactive approach to increased cash flow and value creation, and it is beneficial to real estate owners and investors.

COMMANDMENT 45

Bulk ownership of single-family homes is a low-return business at best, and the business model doesn't work with high operating costs and rising expenses.

THE BULK OWNERSHIP of single-family homes is a low-margin and low-return investment business due to the following characteristics:

- Owning a large portfolio of homes scattered around the country is unwieldy and management intensive.
- Most foreclosed homes need significant rehab and repair work that typically equals 10 percent to 15 percent of the purchase price.
- Management fees can run from 7 percent to upward of 10 percent of the effective gross income versus 3.5 percent to 5 percent for apartments.
- Monthly maintenance expenditures can be time consuming and costly.
- Total returns are well below core, opportunistic, and value-added CRE-investment strategies.
- Disposition of the homes can be cumbersome and time consuming and will usually need to be done in a pool or portfolio structure and at a significant discount.

- Operating expenses average 55 percent to 60 percent of effective gross income versus 40 percent to 45 percent for apartments.
- There are higher vacancy rates of 10 percent to 15 percent versus 5 percent to 7 percent for apartments.
- There is highly volatile pricing of the homes that are subject to extreme interest-rate risk.
- Diseconomies of scale as operating costs increase faster than revenues do as more homes are purchased.

Whenever I discuss this industry with clients or give a CRE presentation, I ask the audience two questions. One is, "If the bulk ownership of single-family homes is such a good business, why weren't there any successful companies in the business before 2009?" Question two is, "What would you rather own, three hundred homes spread across four states or a three-hundred-unit apartment building?" The answer to the first question is that all the firms that have tried bulk ownership have gone bankrupt. (The largest was a company called Epic, headquartered in the Midwest, that owned about eleven thousand homes and went out of business in the 1980s.) For the second question, everyone in the audience always answers owning the three-hundred-unit apartment building.

COMMANDMENT 46

Culture determines strategy in commercial real estate organizations, not the other way around.

A NUMBER OF TODAY's most successful commercial real estate organizations were started by entrepreneurial individuals in brokerage, development, private real estate equity, and advisory businesses. Many of these firms are guided by well-established operating and investment strategies. For example, a private-equity firm may have raised funds from institutional investors and deployed those funds by investing in apartments, office buildings, or distressed debt. Another may be a local brokerage firm that specializes in the sale of net-lease investment projects, and another may be a real estate development consulting firm. As real estate firms grow from one or two entrepreneurial founders, they evolve with an established business strategy and a certain culture. In analyzing the operations of a company, many think that the strategy of the company determines its culture; however, I posit that it's the other way around. The structure or culture of a firm determines its strategy. That is, the culture that becomes embedded in the firm dictates its growth, hiring program, operational strategy, and profitability. This may sound counterintuitive, but it is true in many instances, especially with professional real estate service-type firms.

As real estate firms grow and their strategy becomes successful, they often build up a corporate structure that gets more and more consistent and efficient and eventually rigid. Even though the company is growing and successful, it becomes insular. How many times have you heard executives at a real estate company say, "This is how we do things here" or "It's our way or the highway" or "We only buy core properties in core markets"? This insular thinking and culture and a static corporate structure feed on themselves and are celebrated and codified in the organization. The company then begins to hire only people whose values, points of view, and interests follow the corporate mantra. I faced this issue back in 2005 when I was in a joint venture with a notable investment-management firm to raise capital in a private-placement real estate offering. I was the managing partner of the fund, and my joint-venture partner was responsible for capital raising and infrastructure including office services and support personnel. This company was so inwardly focused that its executives would not approve of anything that wasn't developed internally. It got to the point where one of the senior marketing personnel, who didn't know anything about commercial real estate, wanted me to change the deal slides in a PowerPoint presentation to potential investors. When I said that didn't make any sense and refused, the person stated, "This is how we always do our presentations."

Over time, the employees in these companies seek to protect their jobs, organization structure, and established practices, which further reinforces this company rigidity. Since the company is managed by those who are internally focused and care less and less about developing new strategies, the company does not see or adopt new technologies, business processes, or investment programs and often does not see negative market changes. Think again about the number of real estate private-equity firms, real estate funds, mortgage bankers, developers, brokers, and so on that did not see the coming of the Great Recession of 2007 and therefore did not change or adjust their strategy and continued to make overpriced and foolish investments. Eventually, the company's structure or culture becomes too confining and out of touch with its customers and market that it falters. The structure and culture of a real estate company therefore determine its strategy.

This organizational-culture damage is prevalent in many real estate organizations, especially today. If the CEO or managing partner went to Harvard, then the firm only hires Harvard grads; if the management team came out of the pension-advisory industry, they only hire individuals from that sector. Firms caught up in this culture trap do not want alternative points of view or dissenting strategies. Many real estate firms that were tops in their business prior to 2007 are now out of business, in dire straits, or bankrupt, and one of the overriding reasons is this culture corruption. The remedy for this "culture determines strategy" conundrum is to create an open and diverse organization and culture that encompasses dissenting opinions, new ideas, and outside-the-box thinking and includes individuals with diverse backgrounds and talents.

COMMANDMENT 47

Corporations that own nonstrategic commercial real estate should sell it and reinvest the proceeds in their core business, where the return is a lot higher than in the real estate business.

MANY PUBLIC COMPANIES have substantial sums invested in commercial real estate that they own and use in their businesses. The real estate can be a headquarters office building, industrial warehouse property, retail-store site, or restaurant building. Dillard's and Sears/Kmart, two department-store operators, own many of their own stores. Cracker Barrel, Bob Evans Farms, and Ruby Tuesday, three restaurant chains, also own a large number of their restaurant buildings and sites. Zynga, the online game maker that went public in December 2011, bought its headquarters building in San Francisco's South of Market neighborhood in 2012 for approximately $230 million. Google, a technology company, bought its 2.9-million-square-foot New York headquarters building in 2011 for $1.9 billion.

Commercial real estate is considered a capital-intensive asset and includes four main property types: office buildings, retail centers, industrial warehouses, and apartment buildings. Each type of property (except apartments) is subject to a lease contract that typically has a base rent, additional rent for the payment of property operating costs such as real estate taxes and maintenance, a term of three to ten years, and options for renewal. The base rental rate varies depending on the location and market of the property, age of the building, lease terms, and credit of the tenant.

Does it make economic and investment sense for a public operating company to sink large amounts of capital in its own real estate like Zynga and Google did? Should an operating company own or lease its real estate? From a return on capital perspective, the answer is no. A public company should not tie up capital in commercial real estate, whether it's used for office, industrial, or retail purposes. Companies with large real estate holdings should sell the assets or do sale/leaseback transactions unless the assets are of strategic importance or investment value. Some companies do need to own real estate for strategic and marketing purposes. Examples are a retailer buying a building on Fifth Avenue in New York or Rodeo Drive in Beverly Hills for a new, high-profile store location to advertise its business or a company buying a suburban office building for its national headquarters. In most other cases, the capital tied up in real estate should be reinvested into the company's core business, where the rate of return is higher than in a real estate investment.

The realized return from investing in an operating business is higher than a real estate investment. This is because of risk. Operating-business investments are riskier than real estate investments due to the volatility of the business and industry, difficulty in generating increasing EBITDA (earnings before interest, taxes, depreciation, and amortization), free cash flow and net profits, regulations, and, of course, intense competition. Commercial real estate investments are less risky because properties are encumbered by leases, as stated above, which can deliver a more reliable and steady income stream, and the ability of the lease income and asset to be easily financed.

The best proxy for operating-company investment returns is the return from private-equity-capital investments. Per Cambridge Associates LLC, a financial research and advisory firm, the average annual return for private-equity investments for the ten-year period ended September 2014 was 14.11 percent. The average annual return from investing in commercial real estate can be viewed through data provided by the National Council of Real Estate Investment Fiduciaries (NCREIF), a nonprofit provider of institutional real estate investment data, and the FTSE-NAREIT All Equity Index, which is an index of the return of all public-equity real estate investment trusts. NCREIF provides a quarterly property index that is a time-series-composite total rate of return measure of investment performance of a very large pool of individual commercial real estate properties acquired in the private market for investment purposes. The NCREIF average annual return for the same ten-year period ended September 2014 was 5.44 percent, and the FTSE-NAREIT All Equity Index average annual return for the same ten-year period was 8.53 percent.

The realized return in private equity at 14.11 percent is greater than the NCREIF 5.44 percent and NAREIT 8.53 percent return in commercial real estate. Therefore, operating companies should dispose of their real estate and reinvest the proceeds in their core business. Operating companies should be able to increase their investor return by selling real estate assets and redeploying that capital back into their core business. As an example, a hypothetical operating company, ACME Digital, that manufactures circuit boards and disc drives has delivered an average annual return of 22 percent since going public in 2000. It owns a headquarters office building, free and clear, that was bought for $60 million with a book value of $50 million and a market value of $100 million. If the building is sold in a sales/leaseback for $100 million, the net proceeds after a 35 percent tax rate are $82.5 million ($100 million sales price less the $17.5 million paid in taxes from the gain on the sale). If the company has a weighted-average cost of capital of 12 percent but can earn a 22 percent return (the company's historical return on equity) on reinvesting the $82.5 million in its business, the company will add $18.1 million in value annually to its shareholders. ACME Digital will have to pay rent for the sale/leaseback, which will reduce EBITDA and net income; however, this transaction will result in a higher stock price and enterprise value.

The intrinsic value of a company is the present value of its free cash flows and terminal value discounted at its weighted-average cost of capital. The incremental cash flows generated from the above investment will increase this intrinsic value. If ACME Digital decided to keep the real estate, it would have a slightly higher net income because the deprecation would be less than a comparable rent; however, it would not have the capital to reinvest and earn the incremental 22 percent return.

The capital companies have tied up in real estate is not earning a return other than the amount of rent being saved by owning the property. However, this amount is very small compared with the lost capital investment. Today, many public companies are evaluating their return on capital and asset utilization in a difficult economy. One way to increase these returns is to dispose of nonstrategic real estate assets and reinvest that capital in the business operation to generate organic growth. Companies that reinvest this real estate capital into their core business can earn a much higher return on equity, which will result in a higher stock price and market value.

COMMANDMENT 48

A rolling loan gathers no loss.

THIS COMMANDMENT IS somewhat sarcastic and refers to the difficulty that can occur for a real estate project when the property debt comes due, but the capital markets are in distress and the loan cannot be refinanced. The CRE industry has become very volatile and is subject to wide swings in economic and credit activity. Whenever the economy is in a downturn or recession, the industry contracts with less new development, less ability to raise equity capital, and fewer lenders to provide financing for new or existing projects. There have been eight recessions since 1960, including the two secular downturns, each of which has coincidentally lasted about five years. The first secular contraction occurred from 1987 to 1992 and began in the Northeast and then spread to the Southwest and finally the West Coast. The second secular downturn, as previously discussed and known as the Great Recession, began in 2007 and ended in 2012.

During a deep recession and secular downturn, the CRE industry contracts, sometimes severely. Lenders become extremely conservative in their project underwriting and provide new financing, refinancing, or loan extensions only to select or favored customers, if at all. This lack of debt liquidity is one of the primary reasons CRE projects end up in foreclosure or bankruptcy and is further discussed in commandment forty-four on page 88 . Therefore, if the property borrower can keep rolling over the loan (extension of the loan by the lender), it will gather no loss.

COMMANDMENT 49

The best time to buy commercial real estate is during a bad recession, and the best time to sell commercial real estate is in an economic boom. Many real estate investors do just the opposite.

THE MOST MONEY and higher returns in CRE are made when properties are purchased during a bad recession or secular downturn, such as the one we just experienced from 2007 to 2012 (the Great Recession). During these periods, property values decline precipitously and trade at less than their replacement cost and the income-approach values. This large diminution in value is caused by lower or declining rents, higher vacancies, and tight credit markets. Astute investors who have access to capital can take advantage of these adverse periods by buying CRE on the cheap. Once the downturn ends and a new economic expansion cycle begins, the property rents and occupancy will increase substantially, and the result will be significantly higher values. This investment process is known as value investing or being a contrarian and can be compared with value-investment firms that acquire stocks that are out of favor or during bear markets.

Buying in the bad times and selling in the good times is the best method to make money in the CRE industry. However, it takes tremendous fortitude to buy in the depths of a nasty recession or financial calamity. CRE-investment funds may have institutional and high net-worth investors who become scared and want to redeem all or a portion of their committed funds.

Their modus operandi during the bad times is to contract their business and wait until the economy improves. As of the writing of this book in the first quarter of 2015, the best place to seek CRE-asset bargains is in Europe, where the euro economy is beginning quantitative easing (the central bank is purchasing government-issued bonds) to combat a deep and lingering recession.

Many real estate investors, whether they are small entrepreneurial firms or large institutions, buy properties when markets are booming and assets overpriced and sell properties when markets are soft and values are declining. They would improve their returns substantially by doing the exact opposite—by not following the herd and buying during the boom times and overpaying for property at low capitalization rates (see commandment one on page 1). The most successful CRE-investment firms—such as Blackstone Group, Starwood Capital Group, Loan Star, and others—are contrarians and value investors and seek to buy properties in the down times and sell in the boom times.

COMMANDMENT 50

Many investors and market watchers confuse transaction velocity with commercial real estate intelligence. Just because a firm is buying a lot of property doesn't mean its executives know what they are doing or are creating value.

W̲HEN THE CRE industry is in a boom period and there is a lot of transaction activity by a firm, many investors and market pundits incorrectly believe that the firm doing a lot of deals is really shrewd and knows what it is doing. This is the situation today, with many real estate private-equity groups, foreign firms, and developers buying numerous properties at high values. Just because a real estate investment firm is buying a lot of property doesn't mean its executives know what they are doing or are creating value for their investors. Many times, these firms have plentiful access to debt and equity capital and go on dangerous buying sprees. They often end up overpaying for property because the capital is readily available, and they need to put the funds to work in more transactions. They also may need to acquire a lot of properties to generate various fees to fund their operations, or they are ego driven to be the biggest property owner in a market.

A good example of this buying binge is illustrated by the largest net-lease REIT, American Realty Capital Properties Inc. (ARCP). ARCP is a high-flying net-lease (CRE assets such as restaurants and retail buildings that are net leased to one tenant) REIT that was cobbled together into a $20 billion asset behemoth. In the span of a few years, ARCP grew into the largest net-lease REIT by using cheap debt capital in a dizzying array of acquisitions. In 2013 and 2014, ARCP acquired at least eight large net-lease companies and portfolios totaling over $16 billion at very inflated cap rates of between 5 percent and 6 percent. Net-lease portfolios should trade in the 7 percent to 8 percent capitalization-rate area. The majority of the net-lease deals that ARCP now owns are net leased to retailers such as Walgreens and Dollar General and restaurants such as Red Lobster. ARCP substantially overpaid for all these acquisitions and is saddled with more than $10.5 billion in debt and $1.9 billion in goodwill. Any REIT that is required to book $1.9 billion in goodwill on acquisitions has severely overpaid for those assets. This means that ARCP's auditing firm could not allocate the full inflated purchase price to the real estate assets acquired and had to charge the excess net asset value to goodwill.

Things started deteriorating for ARCP in April 2014, when one of its largest institutional investors sent a letter to the board of directors asking for the company to stop making these large acquisitions so that the financial statements could be analyzed without the volatility of all the deal making. The senior management team was subsequently forced to resign, and a new management team is in the process of being hired. During mid-2014, ARCP disclosed that there were intentional misstatements in its financial statements of approximately $23 million. ARCP has also delayed filing its third-quarter 10Q until April 2015. Due to its overly aggressive growth strategy, overpayment of assets, accounting misstatements, and management turmoil, the stock of ARCP has dropped from fifteen dollars per share to nine dollars per share, or 40 percent, during the last year.

CRE investors and market pundits regularly confuse a lot of deal activity with industry success. This is often not the case, and most firms that pursue this strategy usually crash and burn and end up in the trash heap of high-flying real estate firms.

INDEX

H

Higher and Better Use   4
Hotels   75,76,77
Houston   82

I

Income Approach   28,29,100
Independent Living   75,77
Industrial Properties   7,9,25,39,75,95,96
Inflation Risk   88
Interest-Rate Risk   88,91

J

Joint Venture   15,93
Jones Lang LaSalle   25

L

Lease   14,16,24,32,33,35,46,51,52,53,54,56,66,69,70,81,
                         84,88,92,95,96,102,103
Leasing Risk   88
Legal and Title Risk   88
Leverage   21,42,44,63
LIBOR   74
Liquidity Risk   74,89
Load   20,,21,67,68

M

Management Risk   88
Market Risk   88

ABOUT THE AUTHOR

Joseph J. Ori began his career in commercial real estate in 1981 as the controller/assistant VP of acquisitions for start-up real estate syndicator VMS Realty Inc., SVP of Southmark Corporation, a Fortune 500 Company. He then formed Paramount Capital Corporation and has held senior level positions across the industry, working in finance, investments, investment banking, advisory services, and management. All told, Ori has been involved in over  $3.2 billion in transactions over his thirty-five-year career.

A certified public accountant (currently inactive), Ori is also licensed as a chartered financial analyst. He holds an MBA in finance and is an adjunct professor of finance at Santa Clara University. He publishes *View of the Market,* a monthly newsletter focusing on commercial real estate strategy and investments.

Ori owns Paramount Capital Corporation, a commercial real estate advisory firm, based in Walnut Creek, California. You can visit his website at www.paramountcapitalcorp.com.